Super-Me

A DIY guide to unleash your inner Superhero

Ani Sengupta

Copyright © 2020 Ani Sengupta

All rights reserved.

ISBN: 978-0-473-53509-4

DEDICATION

To my mother, my teachers and guides. Thank you.

Many tools and techniques mentioned in the book are based on publicly available information. Where, a technique has been taught to me by my teachers or guides, I have mentioned their names. Some have been created by me but please feel free to add to them, enhance them to suit your needs. Most importantly, share them with others.

CONTENTS

	Acknowledgments	i
	Preface	1
	Introduction	4
1	Make A Wish	14
2	The Jolly Wally Way	34
3	Don't Patent Your Patterns	47
4	Face or Fall	62
5	Dealing with Emotions	77
6	Karma is What?	88
7	No Escape!	96
8	Accept or Regret	110
9	Resilience	132
10	Finding your True Purpose	151
11	Theory: Complex Web	171
12	Theory: Partner in crime or partners in crime	175
13	Theory: Knock! Knock!	180
14	Theory: The Journey	183

ACKNOWLEDGMENTS

Nicky Moona for believing in it.

Renu Agrawal and Bibiana Vasquez for their guidance and introductions to various healing modalities.

John Jurcik for his support through testing times.

Samantha Bovey for her enthusiasm and help.

Felix Hallwass for his candid and supportive reviews.

Lari Konfidan for introducing me to journeys.

Dawn Raffel for editing the script.

Shoma Mittra and Kevin Barron for taking it to the finishing line.

Andy Kahle for the cover page.

Anirban for illustrations.

Ward Roberts for photography.

And everyone else who has helped me become my Super-Me!

PREFACE

While still in my twenties, I achieved my goal of living in four different countries in Asia, Europe, and the USA, all while moving up the corporate ladder. As I closed in on thirty, I earned my MBA, worked for top consulting firms, and made good money. Yet I suffered from anxiety, depression, a deep sense of dissatisfaction, and restlessness. I had changed jobs, moved countries, made trips to far away exotic places—and while that helped temporarily, the restlessness always returned. By thirty-four, I was married to a stressful job, had waded through three back-to-back failed relationships, ended an engagement, put on thirty pounds, and was diagnosed with diabetes. To the outside world, I was a perfectly normal, hard-working and successful business professional. But the restlessness kept driving me to question my purpose, my actions, my decisions and everything around me. Was this what I was supposed to be doing with my life? I decide to leave. I risked my career, my finances, and my future plans, and against the wishes of my friends and family, bought a one-way ticket to the Himalayas.

For nine months, I devoted myself to studying eastern philosophies in ashrams and monasteries, practiced meditations, and underwent powerful energy healings. I also read widely: everything from Eckhart Tolle's The Power of Now to ancient Vedic texts, Thich Nhat Hanh's teachings, and the latest cognitive psychology.

Nine months later, at twelve thousand feet of snow-capped mountains, amid the echoes of temple gongs, I felt reborn. It was during this time that I developed the foundations of Super-Me. But it took me another ten years to write it, studying energy sciences, meditations, and healing techniques while continuing my career in management consulting, working closely with millennials. I also used my background in engineering and business, and my corporate experiences to design some of the tools mentioned in the book.

Most self-help books take a prescriptive approach by providing rules, principles, and some great ideas for alternative ways of thinking and replacing negative habits. These have certainly inspired me, but I've found that the highs from these inspirations have been short-lived. They have lasted until my next bout of inner restlessness or my next big challenge. They haven't addressed the root causes.

The tools and techniques I've mentioned in this book are based on meditations and cognitive psychology, and are designed to work from the inside out. When we resolve old fears, traumas, and insecurities at their root-level, we heal old wounds rather than simply apply another band-aid.

'Super-Me' simplifies a number of deep concepts and combines an awareness-based approach with some prescriptive suggestions to empower you in a holistic way, so you can make your own transformation, unleash your inner Superhero.

What is your inner Superhero?
The term Superhero as I use it here is about empowerment -- physical, emotional, and mental. Everyone's definition and threshold for 'Superheroism' will be different, and that too is part of this book. My Super-Me or inner Superhero is the guide inside me who helps me find my true purpose in life and align with it.

I have experienced the power of the Universe and relied on

it, using meditation and visualization techniques to remove blockages that I had created for myself. I have shared these techniques in this book. I have learned to identify underlying fears that caused me to experience anxiety and depression. I have shown how simply this can be done by releasing negative emotions. I am not shy about reaching out to experts when I need help. Their input has helped shape some of the tools and techniques in this book. I have learned to accept and love myself and others, balance my expectations and attachments, and find my pace and peace. I have learned to shield myself from negativity. I am my strength, my guide, my guru, my own Superhero and I want to share this knowledge with you. My hope is that this book will help you become your own guide, your own guru. Pick and choose the meditations, visualizations, cognitive and other techniques that work best for you and trust yourself. I hope you are as excited as I am for you. That you are reading this suggests you wish to make positive changes. You're ready.

Who are the Jolly Wallys?
Each chapter begins with an illustration followed by a parable about characters I call the Jolly Wallys. Although they are fictional, you'll find them surprisingly familiar. Some are dogmatic and stubborn while others have a certain simplicity in their wisdom and questions. Some are complacent in their own ways, with interesting ways of interpreting events and actions. They're there to give you a spark of recognition and a smile. It is up to you to interpret the illustrations and parables in your own way.

INTRODUCTION

Hang on! I'm reading about this alien invasion

The Jolly Wally Savior of Humanity

An alien spaceship circled the Earth to scan human brains and understand them better. As it flew over the land of Jolly Wallys, its scanner displayed extraordinary brain activity. The alien immediately landed and found itself on a terrace in front of a Jolly Wally. He was sitting on a rocking chair, sipping tea, and reading a newspaper. The Wally looked up once, then returned to sipping his tea, undeterred.

Alien: Tell me, Earthling, how do you manage such exceptional brain activity?

Wally (looking up): The trick is to think more and do less. What do you do where you come from?

Alien (amused): We focus all our energy on being mindful of our true purpose.

Wally (laughing): We have found ours long ago.

Alien (excited): That is incredible. What is yours?

Wally: To capture aliens when they appear.

The alien stepped back and looked around, but there was no hint of impending capture.

Alien (flummoxed): Are you going to capture me?

Wally: I have done so in my thoughts.

The alien reported back to headquarters. They decided that Earthlings spend too much time inside their heads and thoughts, instead of taking action. Hence, they weren't worth colonizing.

That is how we survived another attack of aliens or so the Jolly Wally wrote to the Government and won an award for saving mankind.

I hope you are not a Superhero in thought-only like that Jolly Wally.

***

How to Use This Book

The first ten chapters outline five comprehensive pillars that make us our own Superhero and offer techniques for developing them. The flow of topics and discussions helps introduce complex concepts in a simplified manner.

After you have read the book, you can use each chapter as individual reference points.

The final four chapters include theories for those interested in esoteric aspects of how we're connected with people, our families and loved ones. It also delves into a theory of the purpose of human existence for the planet. As you go through this book, I recommend you look within yourself and assess your life experiences. A Superhero is introspective and self-aware.

During my journey through the Himalayas, I stayed at a yoga ashram for two weeks, practicing hatha yoga. The schedule was very strict, with specific times for food (mostly steamed vegetable with lentils and rice and lots of peanut butter for desert). It was the peak of summer in April and during the evenings when the sun set, I would sneak out of the ashram to walk around Rishikesh (its name is derived from the term "land of yogis"). On day five, I fell terribly ill with fever—likely from the heat or from eating something bad outside the ashram. I was stuck in my room and survived on water and biscuits for the next three days, getting up only to fetch some fresh water. All I did was sleep and dream. I don't recollect all the dreams, but I remember one vividly, where I saw myself writing poetry. When I woke up, I started to write.

The gist of what I wrote is that all answers I am looking for, lie within me. All I need is to ask myself the questions. A sense of peace came over me as I felt empowered, knowing that I had the ability to guide myself. I was, however, yet to learn the 'how,' through a myriad of experiences, tools and techniques which I shall discuss throughout the book.

I want to share them with you, so you can find your inner powers. This book will help you investigate your behaviors, traits, and inner self so you are able to understand the elements that underlie your behaviors, and begin to align with your true self. My hope is you will recognize that you have the ability within you to heal yourself. That you will be empowered with various tools and techniques mentioned in this book. Teachers, helpers, healers and others will come to your aid when you embark on this path of healing and when you open yourself to the Universe. The more you use the techniques suggested in the book, the more intuitive you will be, in recognizing patterns and determining your path to the abundance you seek.

Pillar 1: Goals and Visualizations (Chapters 1 and 2)
Chapter 1: Make a Wish
This chapter will help you understand how wishes work. It includes a powerful visualization technique and points out some common traps of wishful thinking.
Chapter 2: The Jolly Wally way
The Jolly Wally way is to believe in miracles--but what exactly are miracles? Are they happenstance? Coincidences? Or do you make them happen? Discover the reasons that some of our wishes do not come true and how to use mindfulness and writing techniques to deal with these disappointing situations.

Pillar 2: Patterns and Emotions (Chapters 3, 4 and 5)
Chapter 3: Don't patent your patterns
The secret to breaking negative patterns lies in the power of emotions: those clingy, little things that do not let us go. Harness their power! As a Superhero, you choose the method that works for you: cognitive or meditative. I have used both.

Why not?

Chapter 4: Face or Fall
Our anxieties are connected to our fears, external or internal. External fears have to do with perceived threats like water or height or insects and reptiles while internal fears are related to loneliness, rejection, failure and others. The latter effect our professional and personal lives. I have shared my internal dialogues when trying to determine my underlying fears; I hope you will find them entertaining and useful in helping you identify fears that underlie your anxieties. I also discuss a cognitive visualization technique to help you deal with your fears you have identified.

Chapter 5: Dealing with emotions
While emotions are necessary and important, there are times when I wish they would give me a break. Unfortunately, emotions don't listen to me; but my mind, their boss, does! Learn to quickly deal with your emotions with four techniques. As your own Superhero, you get to pick and choose the ones that work best for you.

Pillar 3: Concept of Karma (Chapter 6)
Chapter 6: Karma is… what?
There are four types of karmas: self-karma, associative karma, and two others I'll discuss later. The concept of karma is just that -- a concept. It can help us understand how we are connected to each other. Irrespective of one's belief system, and whatever the karmic association one might have with one's current challenge, a powerful visualization technique mentioned here can relieve stress and bring clarity, joy and peace.

Pillar 4: Acceptance & Resilience (Chapters 7, 8 and 9)
Chapter 7: No Escape!
We grow mentally, emotionally, and spiritually through conflicts. There is no escape from conflicts, though categorizing them helps me deal with them better. I've found

that the faster I understand the underlying lesson, the faster I move on. The tools and techniques mentioned here are the same as the ones we used to deal with patterns.

Chapter 8: Accept or Regret!

Most people sigh when I mention acceptance. Everyone must go through some level of acceptance in their personal and professional lives. This chapter includes a value-assessment technique to ease the process. This technique can also be used to identify reasons that certain elements may not be working in your personal or professional life. It also helps you determine your own success measures and metrics.

Note: Acceptance does not mean tolerating bad behavior.

Chapter 9: Resilience

Based on my interactions with people from different walks of life and cultures, I've identified three key traits that help an individual be resilient. Here, I discuss those traits and how readers can cultivate them… The way you deal with challenges is what makes you the Superhero you will become.

Pillar 5: True Purpose (Chapter 10)

Chapter 10: Finding your true purpose

I discuss some peculiar and unique ways people have found their true purpose in life, and I encourage readers to use the tools and techniques mentioned, to find their own. The next step is to articulate that purpose, so it becomes a mantra. Every Superhero has his or her own mantra and can use the energy meditation suggested to align with it.

THEORIES: (Chapters 11, 12, 13, and 14)

These chapters suggest a series of theories that are based on my research and my interpretation and understanding of them. These are questions I asked, as I made my way through the journey of becoming my own Superhero.

Chapter 11: A complex web

Why do we meet certain people at certain times in our lives? The answer is a complex web indeed.

Chapter 12: Knock Knock!

Find out the three reasons I was born into my family, the same reasons that you were born into yours.
Chapter 13: Partner in crime or partners in crime?
Why do some of us end up single, perhaps going from one short-lived relationship to another, while others find a steady partner for life? A theory.
Chapter 14: The Journey
Find out why humans are on this planet.

Before you begin your journey, you must open your mind to new ideas and ways of thinking. Use the following positive affirmation:
"I open my mind and my heart to ideas, thoughts, and techniques that will aid my growth and well-being."
If you have said it half-heartedly, say it again, and out loud until you feel ready to begin.
When I first came across energy meditations and visualization techniques, I wondered how they worked. I put on my analytical hat and questioned the concept of energy following thought. I continued practicing the techniques because they made me feel emotionally, mentally, and physically better. At times, it would take a day or two to feel their effects, but there was never a time I did not feel a positive result. I started reading about quantum physics: the energy connections we have with one another and the universe. All of that opened my mind and heart to energy sciences. I hope you will try the tools and techniques suggested; see for yourself how they make you feel.

- Are you someone who believes you have met certain people for a reason -- or do you believe that everything is happenstance?
- Do you believe challenging situations and conflicts propel you toward growth -- or do you prefer to blame someone for causing you pain?
- Do you feel the need to align with your inner self and your true purpose in life to claim your own destiny -- or are you someone who believes your destiny is pre-determined by a

higher force?

Irrespective of how you have answered the above questions, you can avail the tools and techniques in this book to help you grow and attain the abundance you seek. Your journey to becoming your Superhero will be possible if you are open to the concepts and framework of this book. And if you are open to questioning your own beliefs. Be willing to step away from your current situations, and the emotions they drive, and view matters more objectively.

If you are someone who prefers not to delve into the reasons, then simply focus on the tools and techniques in the book. Some concepts are based on Eastern and Western philosophies and use elements of energy sciences. The framework suggested in this book is exactly that: a framework that can guide you toward becoming your own Superhero.

Many of us have been through traumatic events. Life and death situations. Many have had difficulties coping with such events. If you are one of them, I ask the Universe to bless you and your loved ones. I suggest you focus on tools and techniques to help you heal. I hope it will help you find the strength and peace you truly deserve.

Life is NOT about suffering. Our lives have been bestowed upon us to find joy and peace. Suffering is simply meant to highlight negative patterns and lessons, so we can learn from them and find joy and peace. Many of us believe that our lives are more difficult and filled with more suffering than others. Please know that everyone has their own form of challenges. I have had my share and continue to do so, but my attitude toward them determines how I experience life and the type of Superhero I make. What is your Superhero like?

You might ask, How do I know when I have become my own Superhero?

We become our own Superhero in steps. While we are constantly learning, we go through phases of restlessness that prompt us to pause and reflect. This introspection is meant to help us make changes and grow: physically, mentally, emotionally, and spiritually. These phases are the steps that take us toward becoming our Superhero. Only you will know when you're going through one. At times you'll want to stop reflecting and take action, instead. You'll want to use the lessons and growth and accept yourself for who you have become. When you get to this point, you will have taken a step towards becoming your own Superhero.

One such step happened during my nine-month travel through the Himalayas. Traveling, as many of you might have experienced, can be very addictive and joyful, especially when you're free from worries and the daily stresses of work. But after all the searching, studying, realizing and accepting, I got to a point where I needed to apply this knowledge and wisdom to my life and bring it to others who might be interested.

My next step arrived four years later, and it was not an easy one. I left my job. The change had financial implications, but I accomplished the task I had set for myself – finish a draft of another book, which eventually led to this one. During this time, I also decided to try other forms of meditation and healings, beyond the ones taught by an organization I was volunteering for. I felt empowered to make my choices and my decisions and not be led by fear, or rules made by others.

I believe there are diverse ways to achieve one's goals and it is completely up to you which path you choose. The tools and techniques suggested in this book are provided so you can choose what works for you. The intention here is to empower you, so you don't rely on anyone or any group; you can predict and make your own future, the way you want it. Feel free to augment the techniques here with other techniques you find effective. Share them.

Months or years may go by before you feel the urge for another step of growth and change. When you do feel it, through patterns of emotions and restlessness, know that it will take you to your next step.

I use the term 'Universe' throughout the book and I suggest reliance on it, acceptance of its teachings, alignment with it. The Universe' energy is our collective energy and the energy of other four kingdoms of plants, animals (including insects, birds, and fish), micro-organisms, and minerals. Each one of us contributes towards this Universal energy. Reliance on it suggests reliance on ourselves. Some like to place their faith in God, others in prophets, yet others in deities. Irrespective of your belief system, use the term Universe and associate it with your belief system. I'm a believer of energy sciences since I have experienced powerful energy meditations and alignment techniques. I have designed many tools and techniques suggested in this book based on my personal experience with energy science and that of others I have interacted with.

While the initial chapters will introduce you to simple tools and techniques including meditations, these will prepare you to use the more powerful energy meditations and visualizations techniques in later chapters.

2 MAKE A WISH

The Jolly Wally Woodcutter's Wish – Part 1

A young Jolly Wally woodcutter was busy chopping wood in an enchanted forest, when he came across a beautiful genie hiding among brightly-colored flowers. She was trying to escape from genie-hunters. The woodcutter took pity on her and hid her inside his pile of wood until the hunters were gone.

"I've always wished I could see a genie in the woods," he said. "And your beauty is beyond words. What I would not give to be with you."

"Really?" said the genie, blushing.

"Yes. I would love to be with you."

"Alright," said the genie. And with a giggle, she turned him into a toad.

"Why did you do that for?" cried the Jolly Wally woodcutter-toad.

"To be with a genie, one must first learn to be a toad."

"But I don't want to be a toad! Turn me back to a Jolly Wally at once!"

"Why don't you think about it? I'll be back tomorrow evening."

The genie disappeared, and the woodcutter-toad hopped and skipped and took shelter under a giant, glowing mushroom. He thought all night and made a list of all the things he wanted.

When the genie arrived the next evening, the woodcutter-toad said, "I want to be a healthy, wealthy, joyful, and peaceful Jolly Wally. I want to love my worthy wife and two wonderful children."

The genie giggled again and granted his wish. The woodcutter was suspicious but got back his Jolly Wally form. He enjoyed good health, wealth, joy, peace, and love with a beautiful young wife who loved him back. They had two children, but that is not the end of this story.

***

I've made many wishes in my life. I'll discuss a few of them in this book, starting with one I made when I was in college in the US. During a campus recruitment event, I had come across a global firm hiring graduates. My wish was that they would hire me. I pictured myself wearing a suit, making a presentation to a group of executives. Unfortunately, I had missed the deadline for submitting my resume, so I pinned it to their door when they arrived on campus to interview candidates. I hoped they would notice it and ask me to stop by when their scheduled interviews were completed. Companies often did that, so I imagined having time to change clothes. To my surprise, the Hiring manager stepped out of his office to meet me and suggested that I interview with them right away. I was wearing jeans, a tee shirt, a necklace, and a mangle (man-bangle).

Two months later, I had a job with them – and that was six months before I graduated. Along with the job came the reputation of needing a new wardrobe. A couple of years later, I did find myself wearing a suit, as I made a presentation to executives.

During one of my work trips to New York, I wished to live in Manhattan. I visualized driving toward the city, seeing tall buildings on the horizon. Six months after I made that wish, I was awarded a transfer to New York and during my taxi ride from the airport, I saw Manhattan's skyline come up just like I had visualized.

My next job two years later took me to New England. By then I had begun thinking about writing a fantasy fiction book. With long hours at work, it was almost impossible to do. It took me twenty-four fully dedicated weekends (six months) to write the first draft: a hundred-and-fifty pages. The book never got published but because of it, I met an amazing editor who became my writing coach. If I hadn't met her, I wouldn't have written this book.

How I met her is yet another story. I had missed a morning flight from JFK to Denver (for a client meeting), and the next flight wasn't until later in the day. So I parked myself in a café close to the airport. An old friend visiting from out of town stopped by for lunch and we reminisced about college days. I mentioned my book and remember my exact words.

"I need a sign," I said. "I need a sign to figure out what to do with my manuscript."

"You will get your sign," he assured me. "I just know it."

He left and I noticed a quiet man at the next table, typing on his laptop. He paused to think, then continued typing. Then he paused again to read.

"Are you a writer?" I said to him.

The gentleman was a published author, and he introduced me to his editor in New York. That is how I met her. He was my sign.

I must also mention and thank another: an editor with a large publishing house. She was the only person who took the effort to provide detailed feedback on my query letters and manuscript. Under her guidance, I would later publish several short stories.

The Universe listens to us: to our wishes, to what we say, think, and do. However, we don't know what the journey will entail. Our challenge is to be patient and be open to what the Universe provides us. I can understand the view of skeptics who may read this chapter and wonder if I am perhaps a lucky person and that the Universe has been unfair to them. To respond to that thought, I must talk about my maternal grandfather who lived in India. He was brilliant in school but did not pursue college because he wanted to pay off his father's debt. His brothers were studying medicine and other professional courses while he decided to take up a job. He did very well in his career (this was back in the early 1900's) but went through a series of challenges. There is nothing worse than losing one's children and he lost eight of them. Only four survived and my mother is the youngest of the twelve. The oldest son was diagnosed with Schizophrenia at the age of twenty-five and my mother says the diagnosis broke her parents. My grandfather, though a successful man, had spent much of his money assisting his siblings and the extended family. Yet when he needed help, his siblings did not step up. Does that sound like someone who got lucky? Or that the Universe was working for him?

If you asked him, however, what he thought of his life, he would say that he loves having access to the river Ganges and being able to walk along the river every day. He is grateful that his surviving children are following their passion and believe in simple living but high thinking. He is grateful that he has had a wonderful relationship with his wife. He is grateful that he is respected by his children, his family, his friends and their children. He is grateful that he is a man of his word, one who is righteous and true to his nation. He is grateful that he is able to enjoy little pleasures that he missed earlier in his life. He is grateful that he was able to retire early to spend time with his children. He is grateful that he is able to play chess with them, discuss politics, philosophy, history, and literature. He was what I call an optimistic-realist.

It is possible that there were times when my grandfather may have been angry at the Universe. It is possible that he may have been disappointed by life from time to time. Yet he was able to sift through the negatives and see the positives. He was able to go beyond the bickering and complaining about what wasn't working and focus on what did work for him.

To skeptics, I will say that those who appear to receive opulent gifts from the Universe also have their share of challenges. Most successful people have had to deal with failures. The difference is in perspective. If you tend to look only at what has not worked in your life, you will never be able to recognize a miracle. You may even scare away the miracle, if your energy is more negative than positive. And you will keep attracting negative things to yourself. Instead, if you focus on the positives, you will begin to see how miracles come at you. Appreciate them when they do. Gratitude is important for miracles to take place. It is also important for acceptance – of ourselves and others.

You may wish to be a leader of a team and the Universe listens to your wish and puts you on that track. However, this journey may have tough lessons. You may need to deal with tricky situations, and learn to manage people. You may need to remain calm and have patience, to persevere, and be creative. As you go through these lessons, you may lose patience and wonder why your wish hasn't been fulfilled. You may be closer to it than you think, but you give up and make another wish to quit your job. The second wish manifests itself and the job ends. In your next job, you go through a similar pattern again.

Then you question if the Universe is working with you. You fail to recognize that the Universe is trying to fulfill your first wish -- to be a leader. Providing you the lessons you need to get there. Repeating the patterns until you've learned the lessons. So, you can become the leader you wished to be.

A wish may not be fulfilled until one learns all the skills associated or needed for it. For example, wishing to be an entrepreneur requires that we learn to be resilient, to persevere and remain objective through the ups and downs, to be pragmatic and agile, to manage people, and more. Also, note that two people who make the same wish to become entrepreneurs may have very different lessons, because our lessons are related to our current skill-sets and experiences. The two individuals may have very different skills.

A few years ago, I wanted to take up writing full-time to finish my book. But I put it aside to continue work in the corporate world. My work projects did alright, but I did not fit into the culture of the organization I was working for. I had all the necessary skills and experiences to excel in my job, yet I couldn't understand why things weren't clicking. Eighteen months later, I left. Three months after that, I was writing my book, while working on television scripts and freelance corporate consulting to support myself. My wish to finish writing the book was fulfilled -- but not without patience and perseverance. Not without the setbacks and failures I experienced. But these failures are never permanent.

If I told you that your current failure is exactly what you need to get to your goals or objectives, would you be upset that you experienced it? Most of us get so entangled by our emotional responses to a challenge that we are unable to see it as a stepping stone toward our goals. 'Don't patent your patterns' is dedicated to techniques for dealing with emotions that exacerbate our challenges.

A friend of mine owns a creative business, though deep down he also wanted to make films. The Universe heard his wish and he got introduced to a filmmaker at a social gathering. He began discussing his thoughts with the filmmaker. Talks progressed, and he became more involved with finances. However, he experienced challenges, like a lack of structure, lack of processes, and unreliable people. After six months, he wished to quit the film. The Universe fulfilled that wish, too, and the filmmaker cancelled the project.

To get to our goals, there may also be lessons connected with our karmas (other than lessons associated with skills needed to attain our goals). We will cover that in the chapter, 'Karma is... what?'

Take a moment and think of all your wishes that have been fulfilled. Write them down. As many as you can think of. Then make a list of three new wishes you want to come true. Include your bigger goals and objectives. Why wish for a house when you can wish for abundance of health, wealth, joy, peace, and love? Think big! Think holistic!

Remember we don't always know what our wishes entail or whether we are wishing what is best for us...

The Jolly Wally Woodcutter's Wish – Part 2

After the genie had granted the woodcutter's wish, he got very busy. To become wealthy, he started a company and hired more Jolly Wallys. That meant he had to manage them. The more work he did, the less he saw of his wife and two children, but the work kept him busy walking around the woods. And that kept him healthy and fit, just as he had wished.

Then one not-so-glorious morning, the wife found the woodcutter's lifeless body lying on glowing enchanted grass.

He had forgotten to ask the genie for a long life.

***

Ironic! But we don't always know the repercussions or outcomes of our wishes.

Neither do we know what habits, traits, behaviors, attitudes, or values we may need to give up, to have our wishes fulfilled. Remember the global firm I wished to work for? When I started working there, I had no clue what to expect. The first six months were a struggle: trying to adapt to the work culture and long hours, keeping up with colleagues who worked super-fast and super-hard. Though difficult and challenging, these experiences taught me a lot. I learned to manage my time better. I learned to think strategically and to analyze situations better. As I went through challenging experiences, I did question my wish for this job. But I stayed on. I did well, but long hours meant I had very little time outside of work. My wish to work for the global firm was fulfilled but I had to compromise on other levels.

An acquaintance of mine was a single mother of two. She was passionate about helping the sick. Each time she thought about taking up her passion, she came up with reasons related to her children and finances why she shouldn't. One day she was fired from her job. She thought the Universe was being unfair, and her life was laden with conflict, hardship, and misery. She had been struggling for two months when a friend told her about a coordinator position at the local hospital. It didn't pay very well, but she took it anyway. She is now a registered nurse and does quite well for herself. More importantly, she is happy and successful at what she does. To get there, however, she had to cut her expenses, while she worked full-time and studied nursing part-time.

Sometimes, when our wishes may not come true, there is a good reason for it. At one point in my career, I wished to work for a certain organisation. I managed to get an interview with them. It took six weeks to get through the process, and I was given a level of assurance that the job would be mine if I wanted it. I was confident and even mentioned it to a few friends. Six weeks later, I did not get the job. I was disappointed to learn it went to someone with more experience at a lower salary. Shortly after, I heard that the organisation wasn't open to ideas, that the culture was fairly rigid—not a place I would have enjoyed working. I would have felt stifled and stuck. Meanwhile, I landed a different position that was fun and intellectually stimulating.

The Universe always takes care of us. If we have faith in it and a little patience.

A friend of mine felt insecure about her appearance. She constantly complained she could never attract men she liked. When men were interested in her, she wasn't interested in them; and when she was interested in them, they weren't interested in her. Her wish-list of traits in men was short: at the top was faithful and respectful. For twelve months she went through periods of serial dating, along with periods of not wanting to meet anyone. She changed jobs, moved cities, and eventually found a partner. Two of the other men she had dated were known to me; each ended up in failed relationships and marriages. Both had frequently been unfaithful to their partners.

Sometimes our wishes contradict other wishes we have made in the past, creating blocks for them. There is a need to simplify wish-making by aligning them with one's true purpose. This will prevent you from creating conflicting wishes.

We make wishes, lots of them, all the time. We want them all to come true. Let's say you wished for two things and then made a third wish. The third wish contradicted the first one in ways you were not aware of. Meanwhile, the Universe has been working toward fulfilling your first two wishes. The second wish is fulfilled but the first one stalls mid-way since the latest (third) wish contradicted it. The third wish is fulfilled but takes longer, since the Universe had to undo some elements of the first wish (it contradicted).

For example, let's say, you're an artist and you have two wishes:

1) To find love, and,
2) To have your paintings displayed in a prominent gallery.

The Universe starts working on introducing you to potential agents and galleries. It sparks interest with a local gallery and you now need to work toward finishing the series of paintings you presented to them, within a strict timeline. In the meantime, the Universe also introduces you to a lovely man, through a chance meeting at a coffee shop. This man is funny and makes you laugh. He is wonderful, and you can see a future with him. But you don't have enough time to give to him or to the relationship, because you need to focus on finishing your series.

Meanwhile, you make a third wish to see your paintings displayed across the globe. The Universe introduces you to galleries and agents in other parts of the world but that means more work for you--meetings and discussions with galleries, working with new themes and forms. Now you have even less time to give to your new relationship. There are misunderstandings and miscommunications between the two of you, leading to stress. Your partner demands more time and attention. It gets to a point where you can either save your new relationship or meet your deadlines for your series. You also need space and alone time to paint. You vacillate between wanting to spend time with your man and wanting to focus on your art. Ultimately, you choose the latter and your first wish to find love is replaced by your third wish – for your artwork to be displayed overseas, but because of all the dramas in the relationship, you miss the deadlines. You are heartbroken and pour your emotions into your art. The international galleries love the new work and decide to extend your contract and display your work in the next season. The Universe worked in alignment with the choices you made. When you chose your third wish over the first one, it worked toward fulfilling the third one and undid the first. But the vacillation between the two wishes (#1 and #3) and having to pick one over the other caused delays in fulfilling your third wish.

I experienced a similar situation when I chose to move back to the US for a short period of time and gave up my relationship in New Zealand. I do not regret it, but I have had to accept the repercussions of my own choices and decisions, and the wishes I made.

Imagine how often you wish for something. Then imagine how often your thoughts and wishes undermine each other. Sometimes we wish for things that require us to change our thoughts, habits, or traits. These changes might take a good deal of time before the wish can be fulfilled. Do you see the complications involved?

You might meet someone and wish to be with them, but what if you don't yet know that this person has a habit or trait you cannot tolerate? Yet you blame the Universe when this person doesn't show interest in you. You allow this incident to make you feel insecure about yourself. Perhaps it is for the best that this person is not interested -- the Universe is looking out for you. Maybe this person would have been really bad for you as a lover. Help the Universe help you! When you make a wish, wish for peace, wish for success, and a healthy and wealthy, long life. Focus on your true purpose and align your wishes to it. Before we delve into your true purpose in the chapter, 'Finding your true purpose', let's practice an exercise of visualization.

Technique #1: Visualization of goals
Step 1: Sit quietly on a chair with your feet flat on the floor, hands on your knees, palms facing upward. Close your eyes and calm your mind. Allow your thoughts to pass as you take

deep breaths.

Do not fight your thoughts. Just let them pass or disconnect from them consciously (say in your mind, 'disconnect from that thought') and bring your focus to Step 2.

Step 2: Think of the wishes that you wrote down earlier. Visualize yourself having achieved them. Picture what you will look like when you have attained them. See yourself joyful, content, and smiling. Feel how you would feel when you have attained your wish of abundance of peace.

If you wished for wealth, ask the Universe to help you connect with the higher energies of wealth so you can utilize wealth toward your true purpose in life. Feel the joy. Do this from time to time and allow the Universe to work toward fulfilling your wishes.

What not to do:
During your visualization, do not linger or create negative thoughts of what if situations that prevent you from achieving your wishes. These negative thoughts and energies get in the way of our goals.

Do you want to allow them to? Or would you rather consciously let go of these anxieties and let the Universe fulfill your wishes?

I'll discuss letting go of negative thoughts and anxieties in more depth in the chapter, 'Don't patent your patterns', but if these thoughts arise during your visualizations, breathe them out. Say this in your mind or out loud:

I breathe out all my negative thoughts, anxieties, doubts, and fears.

Do not build up stories in your visualizations that feed your ego with pride. Keep your visuals short, succinct, and joyful. Focus on feelings of joy and success not of pride.

For example, if I am visualizing an abundance of wealth and I start thinking about boasting to people who laughed at me or did not have faith in me, then I have let my pride, and my ego take over. I have become attached to the outcome with a lower emotion of pride. Such visualizations do not work because to fulfil them, the subconscious must align with higher positive emotions, not lower ones. The Universal energies also connect with us when we use our higher positive emotions and not those that feed the ego. So, if instead of seeing myself boasting, I focus my visualizations around how I can use my wealth to help make positive changes in people's lives, if I can help parents empower their children, I'm filled with a feeling of joy. In both cases, I'm visualizing wealth. But the latter does not feed a lower emotion, such as greed, jealousy, anger, or pride. It feeds a higher emotion of joy from giving to others. I might achieve wealth and fame, but my focus is to empower people from all walks of life all around the world.

Some people think we can game the Universe by falsely asking for wealth on the pretext of helping others. While the 'method' may be correct in some instances, the intention is not. We are only fooling ourselves. The Universe and your subconscious cannot be fooled this way. When you find your true purpose, using tools suggested in, 'Finding your true purpose' and then visualize an abundance of wealth to help you fulfill this purpose, you will align with your subconscious and the Universe.

I recognized the power of my subconscious mind during my nine-month trip to the Himalayas. I spent a few days in a monastery in McLeod Ganj, a little village above Dharamsala, India, where the Dalai Lama resides. While living in the monastery, we were not allowed to communicate with anyone. No mobile phones, laptops, and not even eye contact with others. We were also not allowed to write or paint. We meditated every day and listened to lectures by monks. The first two days were tough. My mind kept wandering through various events, thoughts and emotions. On day three, my mind calmed. I felt peaceful and centered. I realized that all the emotional drama and unnecessary thoughts were created by my conscious mind. This was the beginning of my work with the subconscious mind and the foundation of many of tools and techniques mentioned in this book.

If your thoughts connected to lower emotions, rise during the visualization technique, consciously stop yourself and allow those thoughts to pass. Breathe them out.

Or say in your mind, "I break this negative thought."

Then return to your visualization and follow your joy, not your pride. Joy is the feeling you have when you give or do something for someone without the motivation of a return. You are doing it not to boast about it or profit, but to feel good about helping someone in need. That is the higher emotion of joy we must feel. Allowing your ego to get in the way will only create more blockages in fulfilling your wishes. When the ego comes in, we subconsciously act and behave differently. The emotion of pride gets in the way of being humble, of being considerate and compassionate toward those who haven't achieved their goals or are struggling with their inner selves. Pride can make us rigid and overconfident. It can get in the way when we have to negotiate a deal for work or when we have to sell our ideas and thoughts. The ego can get in the way of our decision- making because we will be driven more by emotion than objectivity. This does not mean you shouldn't feel passionate about your goals. Find your true purpose and be passionate about it. Be passionate about the path you will take and the actions you will undertake to follow your true purpose.

Some people have asked me why certain wealthy individuals have humungous egos and yet the Universe has showered them with wealth, even though they spew negativity. While it may appear that wealth gets in the way of growth or causes people to become corrupt and egotistical, people become corrupt or delve into lower negative emotions because they water those seeds in themselves. Because they allow themselves to bask in those negativities. Access to wealth may make it easier to access negative elements because wealth attracts potential miscreants. Ultimately, however, it is the individual's decision as to how he or she wishes to utilize the wealth. Individuals who use their wealth for the betterment of humanity and the environment have connected with higher energies of wealth. That is the ultimate goal we must strive for. Wealthy individuals who prefer to remain in the ego mind also help humanity in their own way, by creating jobs and providing for their employees' families.

However, such individuals will likely continue to create negative energies and karmas and delve into lower emotions, if they fail to connect with the higher energies of wealth. There is always a repercussion of creating negative energy and karma and delving in lower energies. As you sow, so you reap!

The question to then ask yourself is whether you wish to attain only material wealth or whether you ultimately wish to gain abundance of health, wealth, peace, joy, and love. The tools and techniques suggested in this book are meant to help you with all of them. Some may want an abundance of peace and joy while others may want love and joy. Regardless of the combination of abundance you desire, this book aims to help you help yourself. The tools I offer will enable you to access your professional skills in an optimal way when you need them.

My hope is that future generations will utilize wealth for the betterment of humanity and the environment we live in. They have the power to connect with their subconscious minds and bring about a positive change in this world.

It is my firm belief that the Universe is constantly looking to give us gifts and abundance, but we must have faith in it. Allow it to take care of us. Make your wishes, visualize them, and allow the Universe to get working on them. Trust the Universe to make it happen while you focus on your actions and not the outcome.

While I worked on this book, I went through some ups and downs. I went through a breakup in my primary relationship. The person I dated had anger problems, was abusive, and became annoyed if I made time to write. We were very different people. After we broke up, I felt angry for wasting months of not being able to write. It took some time to gain perspective on the relationship. When I did, I realized there was a pattern. The Universe was working with me, awarding me experiences so I could write with greater conviction. Some of you may prefer to rely on God, your religion, deities you worship; while others may prefer to rely on themselves. No matter what your belief system, use it and keep your faith. You will become your own Superhero!

Gratitude.

It is in our nature to overlook what we have and focus on what we don't. For instance, parents often wish their children would be more ambitious and achieve more. Often, we forget to show gratitude for what we already have. There is a story that is worth mentioning here:

A Story of Gratitude

A young and apprehensive Jolly Wally said to his mother, "How do you think I will fare in my exams?"

She said, "Based on how you've studied, I do not think you will get the best of grades."

She mentioned a grade lower than what he desired. Alas! She was right. When the results were announced, our young Jolly Wally was disappointed and came in under the ranking that would allow him access to top schools. He blamed his mother, he blamed himself, and went to college in a remote area of Jolly-Wally land. He could have gone to a college closer to home, but it would have been more expensive, and his parents couldn't afford it.

Disappointed, he left for the faraway college, but he did not give up. He felt out of place and cursed his stars. He had applied to better colleges around the country and waited patiently for their waiting lists to be announced. A month later, the list was out, and his name was in it. Excited, he made an overnight journey to another part of jolly-wally land to meet with the admissions committee. Stood in line that was ordered by grades and ranking. One by one, students in front of him were being called. He waited patiently. Hours later, an announcement was made. All seats had been filled.

Disappointed, he returned. For three months he avoided calls from his parents and did not visit home. He studied hard and performed well. He grew accustomed to the lack of amenities, the funny ways of his teachers, strict rules of the dormitory. Within six months, he had lost 20 lbs, studiously worked towards getting good grades, and made exceptionally strong connections and friends that would last him a lifetime.

He was grateful to be there. Grateful for the people he met, grateful for the fun he was having. It was a big lesson of gratitude, despite of not getting what he had desired.

He was grateful and accepted what he did receive. The young Jolly Wally was me.

***

I've had several lessons in gratitude since then. During challenging times, it is difficult to see them clearly, because they are clouded by emotions. But how do we change our negative thoughts? I recommend the meditation and practices below. They are what saved me from my negative thoughts and emotions. They helped me be more open to my miracles.

Meditation #1: Moving from Negativity to Positivity
Key: Energy follows thought and intention. If negative thoughts bubble up during this meditation, do not fight them but calmly disconnect from them. Say in your mind, 'Disconnect from that thought' and then return to the meditation.

If you'd like to experience a guided meditation, please refer to an extended version, available in the meditation section of www.beyoursuperhero.org

Step 1: Sit on a chair with your feet flat on the floor, hands on your knees, palms facing upward and spine straight, shoulders relaxed. Be comfortable on the chair. You can also do this lying on your bed as long as you keep your spine straight. Take a few deep breaths and settle into the chair.

Step 2: Visualize the energy from the Earth's core penetrating through your feet. Feel a pull on your feet as the energy enters and rises through your legs to the rest of your body. Feel the energy move through your meridians, organs, muscles, bone and tissue to all parts of your body and your auras – physical, mental, and emotional.

Remember energy follows thought and intention.

Command the core's energy to destroy and remove all negative feelings, negative emotions, negativities, negative thoughts, anxieties, sadness, grief, anger, all lower emotions, and feelings. Command the energy to destroy and remove any negative entities and waywards.

Take deep breaths and allow the core's energy to remove all negativities from you.

Step 3: Teleport yourself to a higher energy plane of light lemon-yellow sparkling healing energy above the Earth.
The way teleportation works is, one moment you are seated on your chair and the next moment you visualize yourself inside the positive healing energy plane where you are feeling weightless and are afloat. When you look down from this energy plane, you can see the Earth as a small speck of light far away.

Bask in this higher plane and bless yourself with its yellow sparkling light.

Open the energy gateway on top of your head (crown chakra) and allow the sparkling energy to enter. Allow it to mingle with the Earth's core inside you and together, they will destroy and disintegrate all negativities, negative entities, negative energies inside you. You may feel a tingling sensation on your head as you do this step.

Allow your body, skin, tissue, bones, mental, emotional and physical energy to absorb the sparkling yellow light.

Step 4: Thank the universe for helping you heal. Thank it for your life and for all the positives you have received.

Thank those who have helped you in your life. People who have helped you with your school, your work, your relationships.

Thank your family and friends who love you. Thank your

children, your partner and siblings.

Feel the gratitude spread through your body.

Command the energy to open you to miracles from the Universe. Refrain from making wishes but simply suggest that it open your energy to receive positive miracles. It is the intention that counts.

Step 5: Teleport yourself back to your chair from the higher energy plane.

Smile and open your eyes.

Feel the peace within yourself. Feel the gratitude.

Practice #1: Gratefulness

Every morning, when you wake up or meditate, think of two things you are grateful for. This can be gratitude for being alive, for the breakfast you are about to eat. Gratitude for having wonderful parents or friends or family. Gratitude for having a job. If you don't have a job, be grateful that you have your health, your ability to think and to help yourself. If you do not have a bed or are broke, then make your way to a soup kitchen and thank the Universe for the food it has brought to you.

When we feel grateful, we open our channels to receive more. If you want more miracles to happen to you, you must be more grateful for what you already have. Try it!

I went through a difficult time when I moved countries. I couldn't find employment, even though I was qualified and, in many cases, over-qualified. I learned who my true friends were. Visa issues cropped up and shut a few doors. Big expenses creeped up and I felt like I was in a limbo. Nothing I was doing worked. I went through the emotions of fear and anxiety, sadness and frustration, until I realized I had forgotten gratitude. As soon as I changed my thoughts to be grateful to the Universe, I began to see more clearly. Doors began to open.

Practice #2: Gratefulness
A good practice is to acknowledge gratitude when you are happy. When you are taking a stroll in the park and feel at peace with yourself and nature, when you are promoted, when you've won an award, when you receive your pay-check. Make it a point to thank the Universe or any higher energy that you believe in.

A Superhero recognizes the power of gratitude and is a receiver of miracles from the Universe. A Superhero is also compassionate toward those who are struggling with opening their channels to receive.

2 THE JOLLY WALLY WAY

Genie and the Woodcutter's Son

One evening, a genie paid the Jolly Wally woodcutter's son a visit. She boasted that no one could make miracles like her. The young Jolly Wally disagreed, even though he had heard the story of a genie fulfilling his father's wishes. According to him, the universe was full of little miracles, far more than the genie was capable of.

Genie: "You see the beautiful moon up there… Look how I hide it from your view."

Saying this, she cast a spell; thick clouds gathered in the sky hiding the moon. The genie looked pleased. The clouds moved with the wind and crashed into each other causing lightening to strike a tree nearby.

Jolly Wally: "You see that? It is a miracle that the lightening did not strike us, but instead it struck the tree."

The genie laughed.

Genie: "That is because the tree is a lot taller than us."

She waved her arms, and snow came down over the tree and extinguished the fire. The tree instantly froze, cracked and fell on the ground with a thud, missing the genie and the Jolly Wally by a few yards.

Jolly Wally: "You see? That is a miracle! It could have fallen on us."

The genie shook her head.

Genie: "It was our luck that we stood at a distance from it."

She made another gesture and the tree was chopped into pieces, neatly arranged on top of each other. The snow melted and formed puddles everywhere, and a stream of mud glided down the pile of logs. They slipped and rolled down but stopped before trampling the genie and the Jolly Wally.

Jolly Wally: "Thank the Universe for saving us again!"

The genie laughed again.

Genie: "It was that big log in front that stopped the others from rolling."

Saying that, she neatly piled the logs much farther away. Satisfied she had proved her point, she rested her tail on the wet grass and stood akimbo, waiting for a response from the young Jolly Wally. Her tail slipped, and before she could lift into the air, she fell face down on a pool of mud.

Jolly Wally: "Now that is my favorite of all your miracles."

SUPER-ME

***

The Jolly Wally way is to believe in miracles. Why not? I believe it is a positive way of looking at things. It doesn't mean that you not take actions and wait for miracles to happen. Some call it luck, some call it coincidence. I like to give it some magic and call it miracles.

One of the first miracles I can remember goes back to when I was in College in India. It was during final exams. After studying for five consecutive days, more than I'd normally give any subject, I was quite certain I'd ace the test. However, after five days of intense studies, my mind had gone completely blank. I couldn't recall chapter headings. My classmates asked me practice questions I should have known but could not remember. In desperation, I called home. My mother was calm and listened to everything I had to say. She suggested I take a break and study for the next subject. When I brought up the possibility of scratching the paper (not attending the exam), she was okay with it. She had heard the anxiety and fear in my voice. In the background, I could hear my father arguing and yelling. He was furious I was contemplating dropping a paper in my final year of Engineering. I hung up quickly and returned to the dorms. After a long shower and a longer nap, I woke up staring at the wall next to my desk. I still remember the wall covered with bright yellow, white and green posters. I jumped off the bed and began writing on them.

I can do it…I can do it…

I may have written it a hundred times before I mustered up courage to open the textbook again. I selectively studied for the next two days. I was hoping for a miracle. Typically, the exam would comprise of forty marks of theory and sixty marks of numerical problems, but to solve a numerical I needed to understand the theory behind it. If I studied theory selectively like I had decided, it was unlikely that I could attempt a full forty or solve a numerical. Forty was the passing mark for us.

For the first time in the history of the University, the exam had sixty marks of theory and forty marks of numerical. I attempted seventy-five!

You might call it a coincidence or just plain lucky, but I could have given up and dropped/scratched the paper. Instead, I took a leap of faith, mustered courage and put myself out there. I made the effort, I took a chance.

Years later, I was working in New England, and had a crucial meeting with a very important executive in Manhattan at 9:00 a.m. I was to take a train to get me into Grand Central Station by 8:30. In ten more minutes (8.40 am), I would take the shuttle to Times Square and reach my meeting twenty minutes early. When I got to the train station, I realized I had left my wallet at home. I sped through the parking lot and back home. By the time I reached the station again, the next train would get into Grand Central at 8:57. It seemed impossible to reach my meeting by 9:00, and there was no way I wanted to reschedule on such short notice. Being late would be extremely embarrassing, after months of planning to schedule the meeting. I got into the train and felt my heart thumping against my chest. My first reaction was to take deep breaths, touch my chest (heart energy gateway), and ask myself to calm down. My breath normalized, and I closed my eyes and said in my mind: I wish I could push this train with all my strength and energy, so I can reach my meeting on time.

When the clock struck 9:00, I was at the meeting. The train got into Grand Central station a few minutes early, giving me enough time to reach my destination. You might say it was a coincidence the train came in early, and I certainly couldn't have pushed the train. To me, though, this was nothing short of a miracle! I could have decided to drive to the city instead and ended up being stuck in traffic or I could have postponed the meeting, but I didn't do either.

I remember yet another incident I must mention here. I had finished my first year at business school and was busy looking for an internship. This was back in 2002, when jobs for Internationals in the US were very limited. I may have submitted at least a hundred CVs with no response. Disappointed, I decided to visit my best friend and his wife in

Washington, DC. I had limited funds for airfare, so his wife generously let me use her travel miles. I decided I would spend a week with them, then return to College to take up two part-time jobs on campus. On the day I was to leave DC and return to College, I received a call from a top strategy-consulting firm asking me to come in for an interview the next morning. Another close friend of ours had forwarded my resume to the firm and mentioned that I was leaving town. I went for the interview and ended up spending much of my limited bank balance on a suit, a shirt, and shoes. (I was too tall to wear my friend's clothes.) I got the internship.

Some might say I got lucky, but I believe I put myself in the right place in the right time. How often do we shy away from asking friends to help when we are in need? In this case, my friends helped me; and of all my classmates, I was awarded the top internship in my class.

Many years later, when I lived in New Zealand, after a good day at the gym and meeting friends, I realized I had misplaced a ring my mother had given me. At first, I was disappointed then angry at myself. I took a deep breath and let go of my emotions. I remembered I had put it in my pocket while at the gym. Perhaps it had fallen in the changing room. The next morning, at a friend's suggestion, I made a trip to the gym with two copies of a reward poster. I put one on the main board, the other on the mirror of the changing room. Before I left, I ducked down to look under the benches in the changing room. Lying in the corner on the floor was my ring staring back at me. The fact that it hadn't been found or sucked into the vacuum cleaner was a miracle.

Miracles happen all the time, but most of us are so busy with our lives we fail notice or appreciate them. The more you let go and allow the Universe to work its magic, the more you will notice these miracles. Letting go relates attachment to an outcome. It does not mean letting go of actions you need to take. Do your part, and then believe in the Universe's ability to show you a miracle! Let it work its magic for you.

There have been other times in my life when my risks and

actions have not paid off. Miracles have not happened. At such times, I have had to revisit my actions and my plans. I'm someone who generally has delayed emotions when I go through a sudden challenge. But the emotions do set in, just a little later so I use this to my advantage. Here are some techniques I use to deal with my disappointments. The concept here is to find a way to distract yourself before you go into a downward spiral of depressed moods and thoughts.

Technique #2: Laughing

One technique that works for me is laughing at the challenge. This might sound unreasonable and it might not be easy if you're caught up in the emotions of a setback. My emotions tend to kick in a bit later. I am initially numb and go into problem solving mode and then my emotions come flooding in – delayed response. That gives me some time to deal with the challenge.

I encourage myself to laugh and consider that the universe is playing a practical joke or throwing me a curveball just when I thought I had everything nailed. It isn't mocking me but challenging me and I am up for the challenge.

When I laugh, it distracts me from my negative thoughts. If you are unable to laugh at your challenge, try and distract yourself. Watch a good standup comedy to help you smile and laugh.

Technique #3: Thought Replacement

Another technique I have used successfully is replacing a negative thought with an exact opposite positive thought. This requires some practice but if you try it once, you'll be able to do it again and it will get easier with repetition.

Let's assume I'm feeling like a failure. I pause and accept the feeling. Then I think of a time when I achieved something and emulate the opposite positive feeling of achievement. I may even close my eyes and visualize the past positive event: winning an award or being appreciated for something I did well. I try and look for moments when I felt like I had achieved something, and summon that satisfaction.

Negative thoughts may return after this practice--usually they do, after some time. And each time, I try and replace the negative thought with the positive. After a few times, the thought passes. A more advanced cognitive technique for thought replacement is provided in the chapter, 'Don't patent your patterns'. Practicing the above exercise will prepare you for the more advanced method.

Technique #4: Breathing out
Another technique I have used is to breathe out negative thoughts. For each negative thought, I close my eyes and visualize the sun dissipating it. This fairly simple technique may require practice, since our monkey conscious minds tend to bring up negative thoughts from time to time. The key here and in the previous technique is your awareness of the thought. When you sit quietly in a meditative state, ask your subconscious to be aware of negative thoughts and emotions and then let them go. The more you practice the easier it gets to connect with one's subconscious mind.

Some of you may have also practiced the power of living in the present moment as Eckhart Tolle suggests, breathing and just being. Not thinking about future moments but just being present, in this moment... and this moment... and this moment... and this moment...

Two other techniques are mentioned at the end of this chapter and I'll share a number of other techniques to deal with deeper emotions in the chapter, 'Don't patent your patterns'.

Why we may not always get what we want.
Each time a miracle has happened to me, I have been excited and celebrated it. I have come to believe that miracles happen to those who believe in them and are willing to put forth the effort. If you are going through a negative phase at this time, I urge you to practice the energy meditation I have suggested. It will help you release your negative energy, replenishing it with

positivity. Practice as often as you want.

Now, let's investigate why we don't always get what we wish for. Most of us create wishes in our minds... all the time. I wish I had this... or I wish I did that. I wish I lived there ... it is a never-ending list. The conscious mind will always gravitate towards making little wishes. I have learned to focus my wishes on abundance of health, wealth, peace, joy and love but I cannot deny that I too have made several other wishes in the past. There are two reasons that our continuous stream of wishes may not be fulfilled:

Reason 1. Your own thoughts have constantly wavered and pushed you in different directions, not allowing you to fully focus on what you want. (Remember the chapter, 'Make a wish'?). As a young boy, I wished I could be a doctor. Then I watched blood dripping out of my brother's toe, cut by a piece of glass, and that was the end of my wish. Today I'm able to watch nurses draw blood from my arms without flinching.

At some point in my youth, I wished I could build robots. I thought robots were more mechanical engineering than electronics. Many years later, when I applied for a Mechanical Engineering program, I didn't get in. Instead, I was offered a place in the Electronics Engineering. I did get what I wanted: a degree in Electronics would get me closer to a career in Robotics.

My first job after graduating was in Research and Development for an electronics firm. This aligned with my interest in Robotics, but I found the job uninteresting. It was nothing like I had imagined. Instead of sitting at my desk all day analyzing circuits, I wanted to meet people, travel abroad, and work in a fun environment.

Within six months, I got a job with a software company and traveled to Europe and Southeast Asia. That was the end of my aspirations for Robotics, though I continue to be amazed at everything that is happening with artificial intelligence today. In hindsight, Engineering helped me be more analytical, a necessary skill for any business decision. But you can see how my wishes and thoughts have taken me in different directions. I didn't become a doctor to help people get well, but I ended up writing to help people and empower them.

Reason 2. Some of us believe we are not entitled to certain things. I strongly disagree. The Universe is always providing for us, constantly looking for us to align with our true purpose. It wants to shower us with its gifts and give us all the abundance we need. When you find your true purpose in life, you may realize that some of your past wishes are no longer valid. They don't matter to you anymore. It is also possible that if any of those wishes had been fulfilled, they may have even taken you further away from your true purpose.

You may make a wish but there is no telling how long it might take to be fulfilled. Let's say you had wanted to be a successful entrepreneur. You'd need certain skills and traits. If you didn't understand finance, you would need to gain knowledge of the markets. But it isn't as simple as that. You'd also need to take risks and deal with failures. You might need to learn patience. You might need to give up all other passions to focus your efforts on this goal. You might need to change your attitude toward people. You might need to be more diplomatic. You might have to work for many months -- or years -- before you could become the successful entrepreneur you had wished to be. By then your priorities and wishes may have shifted. For the outcome you desire, you may need to forego a relationship that interferes with your goals. You may have to break away from friends or family if they try to block you from your path. You can reach your goal, but there is no telling how long it will take. There are no instruction books or templates that will tell you or show you the impact of your desire on all aspects of your life. You must completely align with the Universe, so it can guide you.

My mother always said The Bhagvad Gita prescribes working toward goals without expecting results. What does this mean? It is natural for us to be passionate about our goals and our creative pursuits, but we must be passionate about the journey and the actions we take to attain the goals, and not be attached to the goal itself. Attachment to the outcome means obsessing and being so emotionally stuck on the goal that we are unable to objectively plan or create alternative routes or actions. Then, when our planned actions fail (as is bound to happen from time to time), we feel a deep sense of loss, and our fears and insecurities prevent us from thinking objectively about our next steps. The sense of failure triggers a range of trapped emotions like anxiety, frustration, depression, and more.

It is a tricky one, this one. Remember, passion for the path and the actions but detachment from the goals. Letting go is a process that requires constant practice. Here are two techniques that I have used successfully to let go of my disappointments due to attachments to outcomes, and to maintain my faith in the Universe.

Technique #5: Mindfulness

One approach to mindfulness involves a 3-step process: pause, acknowledge, and observe. When you have negative emotions or thoughts, you must first pause.

Take a breath and pause your thoughts.

Acknowledge that you have this negative thought and whatever emotions come with it.

Then step out and observe yourself going through these emotions. See yourself from another's perspective, perhaps imagining you're on the ceiling looking down at yourself or watching yourself through a mirror. This allows you to be present in the moment and allow the emotions to pass.

When you pause your mind from thinking and instead focus on how you are feeling, you are accepting the feeling and preventing your conscious monkey mind from creating more negative emotions. The conscious mind is funny like that.

Technique #6: Writing to let go

As a writer, I love this one. Begin with writing this statement:

SUPER-ME

I am writing and releasing all my negative thoughts. There is no other purpose for writing this.

Then write down every thought that comes to your mind. Release your anxiety into the writing. Don't worry about grammar or style, simply allow your thoughts and feelings to flow. Move them out of your mind and onto the paper or computer. When you are done, delete or tear up what you have written. There's no need to read it, and you will feel much better than when you started.

I prefer writing over telling someone about my challenges, since the latter may create an exchange of energy with the listener. If the listener is objective and a professional (counselor), then it is fine but if the listener connects with what you are saying, emotionally, then the listener will be impacted by what you are going through. How we connect with events and information is how we allow them to impact ourselves. Have you noticed how some people download their stress and emotions on to others? It isn't their fault that the listener is unable to listen objectively but instead connects emotionally and is immediately impacted by emotions created in them. The talker has transferred his or her emotions on to the listener and feels better. And the listener now has to process the emotions and figure out ways to let it go.

I recommend an additional step after releasing emotions through writing. It involves writing statements like...

This is not the end of the world for me. The Universe will always protect me. It will always take care of me. It is okay. Everything is okay.
I won't beat myself up over it. This is not the end for me.
The Universe is looking after me. It always does.
I will accept what comes my way and let go!
The Universe is always there for me. It won't let me down. So let go! Have faith. Let go!

Choose what you like from above or write them all.

Make your own adaptations of the techniques suggested in the book. Mix and match and try them all to see what works best for you. This second step helps reinstate positive energy and thoughts after releasing negativities.

No one has it easy. Everyone has lessons to learn, and they are as infinitely various as people themselves. What may be challenging for you may be less challenging for someone else. Focus on learning to let go and rely on the universe to fulfill your wishes. Once you have made your wish of abundance, focus on actions and activities that distract you from thinking about the outcomes. Your mind will keep bringing up the outcomes you desire because the feeling of attaining it is a feeling of joy. That is the key – the feeling of joy. Feel this joy without thinking about the outcome. Feel this joy when you undertake your actions, when you make your plans, when you are progressing on your path. Feel this joy when your actions don't work out, to help you objectively plan to come up with alternative routes. (Note: there is a difference between joy and happiness, as mentioned earlier in the book). Feel this joy to stop your mind from questioning your path. Use this feeling of joy against your negative emotions and thoughts. Use it to energize yourself to be optimistic and realistic. The key is being an optimistic-realist. I shall cover this in more detail in the chapter on resilience.

Another approach that works hand-in-hand with using the feeling of joy is the notion that you are simply the medium for the outcome you are producing and that the Universe is providing for others through you. This is also a humbling experience that cuts through the ego mind. Whether you have creative projects or business ideas, as long as you are aligned with your true purpose in life and it connects with your projects and ideas, you will be able to use this approach. When you do not own the outcome, you will be less emotionally attached to it. Yet, you will take joy in all the steps and paradoxically, the path that will ultimately lead you to the outcome. It is up to you to use this line of thought to have a calmer, peaceful, joyous path to your abundance -- or you can use your conscious ego mind and tread the path of constant emotional turmoil. It is your choice. Of course, all of the above requires practice, and the meditations and tools suggested in this book are meant to help you with that. Fixating on outcomes is a way to try and control rather than trust. Whereas the feeling of joy in actions is a way of trusting the Universe, without trying to control it.

To be your own Superhero, you must learn to let go and believe in the Universe, so it awards you with miracles you need and deserve.

3 DON'T PATENT YOUR PATTERNS

Sorry darling his chip must be emulating Luna's behaviour

The Jolly Wally's Pattern of Alchemy

A young Jolly Wally inventor was so fascinated by the idea of alchemy, he undertook a year of research on it. Meticulously constructing chemical equations, he decided he was going to turn silver into gold. The first experiment led to an explosion in his laboratory, causing him to move his experiment to the empty barn outside. Alas, there was no barn left after the second trial. Disappointed, he began re-thinking his formulation. This was starting to hurt his confidence, and he tried again but in vain. The Jolly Wally was now convinced this was a pattern, like when he had failed in school and on other projects. He wondered why he kept failing in life, to the point where he almost became afraid to try again.

Our Jolly Wally inventor got depressed, and then began analyzing the reasons behind his depression. He realized he was trying to prove to the world he could do something everyone thought impossible. He wanted to do this out of a craving for attention and praise from his family and friends. He needed this attention to reassure him he was smart and successful, as he doubted his own capabilities. He had always felt rejected by his family members, most of whom were fairly accomplished and successful. It was his fear of rejection, and his insecurity that he was not good enough, that caused him to do what he was doing.

After his new-found insights, he decided to give his alchemy experiment one last try. He went up a nearby mountain, away from home and nosy neighbors, and conducted his experiment inside a deep hole he had dug into a dried-up stream. His experiment failed again. Chemicals combusted inside the hole, mud, and rocks flew everywhere. But when the dust settled, a vein of gold became exposed, previously hidden for centuries underneath the rocks of the mountain.

***

The Universe teaches us by putting us through patterns, lessons that our goals and aspirations have brought to us, lessons that our wishes have brought to us. If we don't learn, the Universe puts us in similar situations. The situations may not be identical, but the emotions they trigger will be similar.

Patterns on larger scales can manifest in the form of history repeating itself. When historical patterns, like wars, occur, it is time to understand the reasons behind them. Until we all learn from those reasons, the patterns like wars and pandemics will continue.

One of my friends had difficulty holding onto her friendships. She would become best friends within days of knowing someone, and within the first couple of months, they would have a falling out. She would cut off all relations with them. This pattern continued, and she had a fallout with me, too. Instead of trying to figure out why she was going through the pattern, she preferred to blame it on the people she was meeting. If everyone you meet seems wrong for you, then you need to look at whether the challenge lies within you.

There is one exception however: when you are going through the process of removing negative influences and people from your life. In such cases, it is possible that the Universe is suggesting you disconnect from many of the negative people around you and connect with more positive influences.

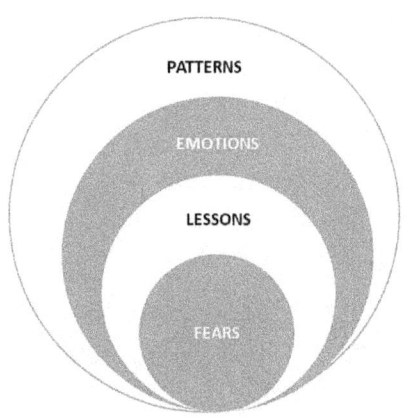

The emotions we feel in our patterns can lead us to understanding the underlying lessons and fears. When we deal with the fears and learn the lessons, the corresponding patterns are broken.

The figure above shows the interconnectivity between our inner fears and insecurities and the patterns we go through. The faster we learn from our patterns, the quicker we break them and get ready for the next lesson. Understanding what you must learn from a pattern is hard work. To understand, one must analyze the pattern and the emotions it drives. One must be introspective and use one's judgment. No one else can solve the puzzle for you but I have provided the tools and techniques you need to solve it.

A few simple questions can help you determine whether what you are experiencing is a pattern:
- How often have you felt this emotion in the past four weeks? In the past three to six months?
- When was the last time you were in a similar situation? Did you feel the same emotions?

To understand what the pattern is trying to teach you, use the following questions:
- How did the situation make you feel? What emotions did you feel?
- Why did the situation make you feel those emotions?
- Is your above reasoning correct? Or could there be other reasons for you to feel the way you did?
- What happened earlier in the day or yesterday or a few days ago that may have fueled these emotions?
- When have you typically felt this emotion in the past? Under what circumstances?
- What are you afraid of?
- Think back to your childhood. Can you remember an event or situation that made you feel the same emotions?

Our negative emotions are often driven by fears and insecurities linked with our childhood. Many of us forget our childhood days, but if you dig deeper, you will find the link.

I once got stood up by a friend because he had a client event at the last moment. I had declined attending an office gathering of my own so I could meet him. It annoyed me. This was not the first time we had scheduled something and he had changed plans. It seemed like a pattern with him.

I ended up attending my office function, but I felt like a

stranger among my colleagues. I felt uneasy and thought I was being ignored. I felt shy. My conversations were short. I wondered what was going on.

Here is the two-step process I used to analyze my situation.
Step 1: Analyzing patterns and underlying fears

As I walked home, I asked myself a series of questions:

Why did I feel out of place at the office gathering? Why did I feel like I was inside a shell?

A: I don't know. I can be introverted sometimes but I do like to talk to people.

Then why did I feel like I was shutting down?

A: It felt lonely somehow, and I felt rejected. That's it. Rejected.

Did anyone do or say anything to make me feel that way at the gathering?

A: No.

Then why did I feel that way?

A: I don't know!

Why was I suddenly so sensitive about how people reacted to me? Did they sense I was uneasy?

A: No one said anything bad to me. If anything, they were trying to be witty and funny. I smiled and laughed but didn't really participate. Maybe I am shy?

It is normal to feel shy if it is a new group of people. Was it a new group of people you did not know?

A: I knew half of them, so it wasn't like I was a complete stranger.

When have you felt this way before?

A: When I have been low energy or disappointed.

How do you feel when you are disappointed?

A: I shut down and don't want to socialize.

Did someone say something at the gathering that triggered some kind of disappointment?

A: No.

Then what triggered it?

A: Maybe it was being stood up by my friend.

How did that make you feel?

A: It made me feel rejected and let down. It made me feel lonely.

Is that how you felt in the gathering?

A: Yes. They were similar emotions.

When have you felt like this in the past?

A: Lots of times.

Can you think of your childhood when you have felt this way?

A: No. I wasn't a shy kid, and I had a lot of friends.

Look deeper into your childhood. Did your friends or family make you feel that way? Any incidents with your friends or family? What's the first incident that comes to your mind?

A: I must have been seven or eight. There were two boys my age who lived in the same community. They were always setting up play-dates at their house. I was rarely invited. I would walk to their house calling for them, only to realize they were hiding inside with others, seemingly trying to avoid me. They would peer from the windows or whisper through the door. I would ask to join but leave disappointed. It was that exact same feeling of rejection and loneliness.

So, do you now know what fear triggered the emotion?

A: Yes. My fear of loneliness. My fear of rejection.

Why do you think the boys did that to you in your childhood? Why do you think they wouldn't invite you to play with them?

A: I don't know. They had done the same to other kids, too. One of them had an older brother who bullied others and worse.

Isn't it normal for some kids to show disapproval by not wanting to play with someone?

A: Yes, absolutely and I'm sure all kids go through some level of rejection in their growing years. I have retaliated to being bullied by behaving badly with others myself. But now I know what triggers my emotions.

How do you feel about it now?

A: Better.

Why?
A: I feel like I understand where this is coming from.

Step 2: The next step for me was to dig deeper into the fears; to understand the lessons I was meant to learn. To do so, I used the following questions:

Were you taking things too personally about being stood up? Perhaps your friend had no choice and felt apologetic. Did you ask him?

Are you making assumptions about how others react, think, or judge you?

If you had given your friend the benefit of the doubt, how would it have changed the way you felt?

If you went through the same situation again, what could you do differently to not trigger your fears?

I realized I needed to heal myself from the fear/insecurity in my childhood. I also needed to learn a few lessons such as:

Staying objective and not taking things personally. My friend who cancelled last minute didn't mean to hurt me, and he did leave a message to apologize.

Giving others the benefit of the doubt. Maybe my friend is terrible at planning and is disorganized. Maybe he had more important things to do related to his work. Maybe he was under pressure or stressed and didn't want to bother me with it.

I must always talk to the person who made me feel the way I did, instead of internalizing and making assumptions. Get more data.

Not blame others for how I feel. At the social gathering, I was probably projecting my own emotions onto others.

Not being too hard on myself. Love myself unconditionally.

Our lessons can be at multiple levels. For simplicity, we'll explore three levels: low, medium, and high. Let's say my lessons are to be patient and compassionate. A low-level signifies I am always impatient, showing no empathy or compassion for others. A medium-level denotes I am generally patient and compassionate, but it depends on my emotional state and mood. If people view me as an impatient person, but I believe I am patient, I would place myself at the medium-level. If I am generally a patient and compassionate person, then I am at a high-level.

Let's assume I have attained a medium status on being objective, but I need to get to a high status before I'm ready to reach my goal of making a leader. I may have attained a low in giving others the benefit of doubt, but I need to be at a medium to deal with my fears. We will never know the exact level we must reach for each skill or trait to get to our goals but we can strive to get better and rely on the Universe and ourselves to keep us going. Try and make the lessons part of your journey, and appreciate yourself for the efforts you put in. Reward yourself, even spoil yourself when you need to. We all deserve it. Once you have identified underlying fears that lead to your patterns, you can use one or both techniques mentioned below to break your pattern.

Years later, I was in a similar situation again where I attended a big party of over two hundred people from different parts of the country. I was a little underdressed and did not know many people. I felt out of place. I sat at my designated table and watched people, nodded and smiled at those I knew. I felt neglected and ignored, even though the people at my table were friendly. It was that same feeling of rejection. For a few minutes, I assessed how I felt, accepted it, and allowed it. I remained seated and nibbled aimlessly at the appetizer. When I was done assessing and before the main course arrived, I decided to break the spiraling emotion. I stood up not knowing what I was going to do and aimlessly walked over to the table all the way across the room. I took the physical action and initiative. Once I was at the other table, I had no choice but to smile and introduce myself to everyone in the other table. There was no looking back. My mind was preoccupied with making conversation instead of wallowing in my self-created feeling of rejection. I had a great time socializing. If you are introverted you know what it's like to force yourself into conversations with strangers. If you cannot start with a table full of people, start with one individual and make your way to a table, when you are ready.

This experience solidified my belief that the energy we project is the energy we receive. Certain events may trigger negative energy we project but it is up to us to be able to recognize this, accept it, and take necessary steps to change it – to make it positive from negative. The same people who I thought were neglecting me or not being friendly at the party were suddenly walking up to me to talk after I took the first step.

I am now mindful of my emotions and my energy. I am more aware of who I am and how I feel. I understand there is no excuse for laziness and the fact that "I" have the power to change things for the better for myself. I am empowered and I am my own Superhero.

Here are two effective techniques to heal us of our childhood traumas and break our negative patterns. The first technique was suggested to me by my teacher and holistic health coach, Renu. It is based on Doris E Cohen's work and techniques. The second one uses cognitive methods for replacing of negative emotions with positive affirmations. Let's use the example of my experience at the office gathering and my fears of rejection and loneliness to explain the first visualization technique.

Technique #7: Self-love visualization to heal from past patterns

Step 1: I close my eyes and visualize myself in one of my favorite spots: a white-sand beach with a beautiful, blue ocean. I see a wooden bench facing the water. I walk to it and sit down. A cool breeze sweeps past me and I feel joyful and peaceful. I take a few deep breaths as I relax into the bench.

You may choose a different location, but you can't go wrong with an open ocean with beautiful blue water.

Step 2: A few yards from me, I see myself as a young boy of eight.

He looks sad and is feeling rejected and lonely. I smile at him (me) lovingly and invite him to join me on the bench.

He walks over to me and sits beside me.

Step 3: "I am here for you," I say to him.

"I love you," I continue, "and you have nothing to fear. You are not alone."

I put my arms around him.

"I am always with you no matter what happens. You will always have me." I continue to reassure him. To make him feel loved and secure.

You may feel sad and cry during this step of the exercise. It is okay to release the trapped emotions. Allow yourself to go through the release. Keep giving yourself self-love and saying loving words of reassurance to your young self.

When the young boy feels better, he smiles at me. His healing process has begun. He asks me who I am, and I tell him the truth – I am you. Look how big and tall you will be when you grow up. He smiles happily.

"But your hair?"

"Yes, you will lose it all, so better take care of it now. But we don't look bad with a shaved head, do we?"

The young boy laughs. (A little humour does help with the healing)

"Will you come here again?" he asks.

"Always! I will always be here for you. Whenever you feel alone or sad, remember I'm with you. All you need to do is to call for me."

My young self, smiles at me happily and hugs me. As he leaves, I open my eyes and feel a sense of peace inside. Take your time with each of the steps and allow your subconscious to guide you through the connection with your young self.

This is a simple yet powerful technique to not only help release trapped emotions, but also give yourself self-love, an important ingredient to healing. The technique may need to be repeated a few times before the trapped emotions are fully released from an event.

It is normal for everyone to go through depressed moods, but if you suffer from clinical depression, it is important to seek external help. Depression keeps people away from their true potential. It keeps you away from taking action. The earlier you seek help, the faster you will be on your journey to become your Superhero. You may have heard the expression we learn when it is time for us to learn. We may hear words of wisdom, other's experiences and advice, but unless it is our time we do not truly learn. The time in this context simply means you may have additional lessons and experiences to go through before you are in the right physical, mental, and emotional state to grasp what is being discussed. If you are reading this book, then clearly it is time for you to be aware of the concepts in it. Time for you to think and assess your life experiences, your goals, and your true purpose.

Have you ever met someone who reminded you of negative traits of your partner or a parent or sibling? Such people bring back memories; they instigate emotions from the past. Are you constantly meeting people who bring back similar emotions? Then it is a pattern and the Universe is hinting to you to look into it. It is suggesting that you find your underlying fear and deal with it. It may be a lesson of acceptance, compassion, forgiveness, or patience. If you think you can avoid the lesson by running away or turning away, know that there is no escape. The Universe will send you more people with similar dynamics and you will have no choice but to deal with them. It is up to you how long you wish to extend your pattern.

Meditation #2: Advanced visualization with cognition
This is a technique that you can use after using 'Tool #1' – after you have identified any negative patterns you wish to break.

Pre-Meditation Work: Identify three events in the past that have caught you in the pattern related to a particular emotion you feel. This emotion may be anxiety, anger, panic, depressed mood, sadness, feeling lonely, fear of rejection or others.

I recommend picking events that are different but cause the same emotion in you. For example, I may feel anxious and fear rejection when my partner is not giving me the attention I seek. I may feel anxious or feel rejected when I am not invited to a party by friends or work colleagues. I may feel anxious and fear rejection if I don't hear about a job that I applied for. These events are very different but all three cause me to feel anxious and fear rejection. The more diverse the events, the greater the reach of this technique.

For example, I can pick the following three events, being bullied at age eight, being stood up by my friend and attending the gathering, and not hearing from someone I'm dating for days. These happened at different ages but all three are connected to my fear of rejection and loneliness.

You may also pick the same type of event. For example, if you have had three heart-breaks and each have caused you sadness, you could choose all three heart-breaks as your events and break your pattern for sadness associated with relationship breaks.

The intention of this advanced meditation is to visualize yourself unaffected by events that had previously caused you negative emotions and patterns. You will be better able to deal with such events in future, remaining calmly aligned with yourself and undeterred from your path. Feeling emotions is normal and these techniques are not meant to make you unemotional towards events that cause emotions. But they are meant to help you deal with these emotions better and faster. With practice, the pace at which you can deal with your emotions will significantly improve and you will be able to take a more objective approach to challenging events in your life and break your patterns. Taking an objective approach will also enable you to you keep to your path of true purpose.

Step 1: Get into a meditative state.
Sit on a chair with your feet flat on the floor and spine straight,

shoulders relaxed. Hands on your knees with palms facing upward.

Visualize the energy of the Earth's core entering through the bottom of your feet and traveling through your legs to your hips and upper body. You may feel a pull on your feet.

Flush yourself with the core's energy. With intention.

Command it to destroy, disintegrate and remove all negativity, negative energies from your physical, mental, and emotional energies. This connection with the core of the planet also helps keep us grounded throughout this meditation. It is important that we are grounded.

Step 2: Next, teleport yourself to the plane of abundance high above the Earth. The way teleportation works is, one moment you are seated on your chair and the next moment you are inside this energy plane. You do not visualize flying from one point to the other.

For those who are more visual, you can see this higher plane with light lemon-yellow energy laced with patches of light violet (based on my visuals of the energy planes). Feel weightless and float inside this energy plane. Bask in it. Absorb the energy through your crown chakra (on top of your head) and through your skin, into your muscles, bones and tissue. You may feel a tingling sensation on your head.

Allow yourself to absorb the abundance of joy, peace, health, wealth, success, and love.

Step 3: Remain inside this energy plane of abundance. Visualize feeling calm, joyful and centered, undeterred by anything or anyone.

Bring up the first event in front of you, as if you are watching it on a screen. Watch the people associated with the event tell you things that caused you anxiety or whatever negative emotion you are dealing with. If it wasn't a conversation, simply visualize a series of activities that triggered the negative emotion. If the event is too traumatic to re-experience, simply visualize the person/s who caused you the negative emotions standing in front of you. Do not recreate the event if it is too traumatic for you. In that case you can practice this in the presence of a coach/counselor.

See yourself undeterred and unafraid by the person/s, the conversations, revelations or events taking place. Smile and feel your inner strength kicking in as you remain calm and watch. You are no longer angry because you have fully detached from the event and the people in them. Take deep breaths. Feel the strength of your calm and peace within. Next feel sympathy and compassion for those involved because you understand that they have caused you negative emotions and thereby negative karma with you and perhaps with others. They do not realise that this negativity will return to them in other forms. You may remain in this state for as long as you want, feeling strong, calm, peaceful, and centered. When you are ready, walk away from the visual -- toward an open door filled with bright sparkling lemon-yellow light, laced with violet colour – the energy of abundance. You enter the doorway and experience the infinite abundance of love, peace, joy, calm, health, and wealth. Remember, energy follows thought and intention.

Repeat this step for the other two events. At the end of the third event, remain inside the doorway of abundance. Stay there as long as you like. Feel the joy and peace of healing yourself. Thank the energy planes and healing guides for enabling your healing. When you are ready, teleport yourself back to your chair. And feel the calm, peace, joy and love settled inside you.

Next time you are in a similar real-life situation that causes the same emotional pattern you had chosen to break above; see how you react. It can sometimes take one to two days to notice the impact of the above exercise, depending on the depth of trauma and trapped emotions you needed to release. Some may feel bouts of emotions for a couple of days and if you do, release them. Allow them to pass. It is part of the healing process.

Revisiting a trauma can bring up feelings that have been buried deeply for many years. Please be wary: This exercise will likely elicit an emotional response; some may even cry; but don't be afraid to face them. By crying, you are simply releasing the trapped emotions and traumas. For those who find facing their past traumas too overwhelming, I recommend you find a therapist or counselor. Talk to them about the above technique and seek their advice. Perhaps they can guide you through the exercise.

The Universe empowers us with everything we need to break a pattern. All we need to do is to ask for guidance, whether we do so through meditations or reach out to our coach/counselor.

SUPER-ME

4 FACE OR FALL

SUPER-ME

Olly – The Fearless
There was once an old wise Jolly Wally that everyone called 'Olly.' No one knew how he got that name, but it stuck with him. His job was to help the younger Jolly Wallys conquer their fear. They came to him from far and wide, all ages and sizes. Our Jolly Wally woodcutter's (from previous parables) widow too sent her teenage son and daughter to Olly.

Every morning, before school, the group of young Jolly Wallys would gather around Olly to find out whether it was their turn to face their fears. Olly would announce a name and lead the person to his or her challenge, while the others watched in horror.

"Are you ready to face your fear?" said Olly to the woodcutter's son that morning.

The young Jolly Wally nodded and followed Olly into a dark cave.

"You know the rules," said Olly. "Ten Wally minutes inside the cave and bring me the shining gem. It is placed on a rock at the center of the cave."

Our young Wally took a deep breath, clenched his fists, and walked in. Sounds of water dripping echoed through the cave, bat eyes glowed in the darkness, and the cave smelled of their poop. The young Wally took cautious steps with a torch in hand, being careful not to step on snakes and scorpions. A sudden screeching sound startled him and his torch slipped and fell. The light wouldn't come back on and the screeching sound echoed again, this time closer to him. The Wally, who was afraid of the dark, screamed and ran out of the cave as fast as he could.

"There's a creature inside… and my torch broke," he said panting.

Olly smirked. "Looks like you have failed," he said, shaking his head.

"But the creature?"

"There is no creature inside, it is the fear in your head. Alright everyone, off to school you go. Let's hope we have a better day tomorrow."

The next morning, it was the young Wally's sister's turn and she was afraid of anything slimy. Olly smirked as he called out for her and ushered her to an old dilapidated and roofless house, covered with slimy green moss.

She entered barefoot with a crumpled face as she felt the slimy moss underneath her feet. The moss was wet from rains the previous night and she slipped. Olly heard the thud and grinned.

"Looks like your sister won't make it," he snickered and shook his

head.

But she stood up and continued to the center room of the house, taking cautious steps to reach the gem. Just as she was about to enter the room, buckets of slime poured all over the floor. It smelled fishy and disgusting. She held her nose and reluctantly took a step on the slime.

"Owww!" everyone outside heard as she slipped and fell again, covered in the smelly slime.

"Yup," said Olly. "Okay, show's over. Off to school now. Go help your sister," he said to her brother and then left in a hurry.

The young Jolly Wally rushed inside and helped his sister out of the broken house.

"I'm going to talk to him for bullying us like this," he said to her angrily and rushed behind Olly.

"Wait for me!" said his sister and limped behind him.

The young Jolly Wally siblings spotted Olly from a distance and followed him into a large building. It was deserted with cracked white walls and old portraits hanging from them. A long corridor led them to a room where the Wally's spotted Olly. He was seated in a group of Jolly Wally's discussing their fears, but he wasn't the one running the session. He was a participant!

The next morning, the group of young Wallys made their way to see Olly again.

"Here he comes," announced one of them.

"So, whose turn is it today?" said Olly with a snicker.

Before he could say another word, the young Wallys presented him with their furry pets.

"It's their turn," they shouted in unison.

Olly jumped and screamed and ran as fast as he could. He was a member of the 'Furry Pet phobia Anonymous.'

***

All of us have fears, even the most successful person. It is the ability to face and conquer fears that makes us our own Superhero. To do so, one must first understand the underlying fears that cause our emotions of anger, frustration, anxiety, and sadness. These fears cause self-doubt and bring 'what-if thoughts to our minds. These 'what-if' thoughts can make us impatient and cause us to take hasty actions that can keep us from attaining our true goals. So, to attain our goals, we must learn to deal with our fears.

I like to start with categorizing fears as internal and external. External fears relate to height, space, water, reptiles, insects, and other factors outside of ourselves, while those related to self, such as fear of rejection, loneliness, abandonment, rejection, trust, and failure are all internal fears.

External Fears

A few years ago, I decided I wanted to conquer my unnatural fear of heights, so I took every opportunity to enter tall buildings and skyscrapers and look down from their higher floors. I made trips to the Empire State Building in New York. It is normal to feel uneasy when looking down from an open terrace or balcony of a tall building but when this uneasiness causes you to not look down at all or to steer away nervously from any location that may be a few stories high, then you are dealing with an unnatural fear. My trips to these tall buildings helped me conquer my unnatural fear of heights -- to an extent.

In another instance, I was hiking and rock climbing in Slovenia. I had climbed three quarters of the way when I stopped, unable to find a crevice or rock to hold onto.

"Look around you," shouted the guide from below.

I stretched my long arms and moved a few steps, but I was over a vertical rock surface with very little to hold.

"Keep looking up," shouted the instructor and I glanced down instead.

Suddenly, my breath hastened, and I felt queasy in my stomach. I remember my hands shaking and feeling a little cold. I was harnessed, so there was no real danger unless the ropes gave way. But I stood there and stared blankly into the sky.

"Keep going," I heard the instructor again.

I closed my eyes and took a few deep breaths. As per

instructions given, I focused on my navel, my heart, and the point between my eyes, and breathed into all three points simultaneously – with intention. When I opened my eyes, I miraculously found rocks perfectly placed within my reach. I made my way to the top.

In my panic, I had failed to see the rocks. This is an example of how our energy determines what we see and attract to ourselves. As soon as I changed my energy and calmed my senses, I was able to find my path. The calmer our minds, the clearer our vision. The more objective our thoughts, the better the decisions we make. My fear of heights did not go away with this episode of rock-climbing, but I learned to cope with it to an extent. I had found myself a technique of breathing into my heart, navel and ajna (point between our eyes) that I could use in future.

A friend suggested skydiving and I thought that it would be the perfect opportunity for me to face my fear of heights again. I won't deny it was nerve-wracking to be standing in the hangar, waiting to board the little airplane that wobbled in air. I'm not scared of turbulence. The scariest moment for me however, was when the airplane reached a few thousand feet and I waited next to the door to jump off. Seeing the person in front of me disappear underneath the airplane was when panic struck.

"Ready?" shouted my instructor just then.

I don't think I nodded or responded to him, but I remember feeling a push and being out in the air, feeling the wind on my cheeks and an eerie stillness as I fell towards the ground.

Yet...I loved it!

Would I do it again?

Absolutely! Despite the feeling of tiredness after the adrenaline rush, which felt like I had been running for days without stopping.

I continue to feel a little uneasy when I look down from tall buildings or towers, but that is natural uneasiness all of us face. I believe I have conquered my fear of heights!

I can swim (some might say not very well), yet I fear open water. After years of trying to overcome this fear, I decided to take up sailing. That's right. It felt like the right thing to do – push myself into open water. Before I took it up, I had taken swimming lessons. A good friend of mine, noticed that my strokes suddenly became weaker as soon as I got to a point where my legs could no longer reach the bottom of the pool. He said that it was clear to him that the problem was in my mind. This was a very interesting observation for me and made me realize that it was the fear in my head that was preventing me from swimming properly. This understanding led me to push myself to deal with this fear and take up sailing.

One of the first lessons in sailing had to do with recovering from a capsize. On the morning of the drill, I felt queasy, but assured myself that I could do it. All I needed were two hours of bravado. I reached the sailing club and walked up the ramp where my mates stood in a queue; wetsuits on, hands folded, excitement in their eyes. I was blinking constantly while I let out bouts of muffled laughter to cover up my nervousness. When it was my turn, I realized that the challenge for me had less to do with recovering from a capsize than pushing myself into the water in the first place. My classmates knew about my fear and cheered me on. The whistle blew, and I found myself pulling the trims attached to the mast. It moved sideways, and the dinghy tilted, throwing me overboard. I remember feeling a sudden panic as I fell into the freezing water. Swimming around to the other side, I grabbed the dagger board before the dinghy could fully overturn. It was now floating sideways. Pushing the dagger board down with my arms I stopped the boat from turning any farther. Then I grabbed the side of the dinghy and pulled it toward me. The boat turned and the mast lifted from the water. My heart did not stop pounding until I returned to the shore, but I felt happy that I was able to manage my first capsize.

The following week, the instructor suggested I slide off the dinghy during our practice sail and float away from it. Allow myself to feel the water around me, get comfortable with it. I had a life jacket on, so I wouldn't drown but as I lay on my back, fears raced through my mind. What if a shark attacked? It didn't matter that no cases of shark attacks had been reported in the bay. I imagined weird creatures loitering underneath. Through this course in sailing, I did not overcome my fear of open water, but I learned a great deal about myself and some techniques to cope with my fear. It takes time to overcome fears and one must be patient with oneself. Just as one must be patient with others trying to conquer their own fears. What may seem to be an easy task for someone may be difficult for another due to an underlying fear. In such circumstances one must learn to help the other person and support him or her through the task.

For those who fear reptiles, I would not suggest you spend a day playing with them, especially if they are poisonous. But if you do muster the courage to visit a pet store with non-poisonous snakes, do it! Walk through the store, if nothing else. Next time, if you feel more courageous, stop and take a peek at a few of the snakes. I'm with you on snakes, though. They are not my favorite reptiles.

Some may fear spiders and jump at the sight of one. Unless they are threatened, spiders don't usually attack. The simple exercise of capturing one in your home with a glass tumbler and releasing it outside might help with your fear.

External fears are best dealt with by taking small steps toward them head on. As long as you're aware of your fear and make it a priority to face it, you will. I also know that most of us will back out of such opportunities. Asking the Universe for guidance to help you overcome your fear is the way to go. Do it while you meditate using the techniques suggested in this book. Command the healing energies to release you from your specific fears.

Internal Fears
I did not realize that I feared failure until I experienced it the second time, at one of my jobs. This was after my trip to the Himalayas. I had returned from nine months on the mountains

and was ready to take on my next challenge. I took up a job but culturally, I did not fit into the organization and the work was very different from what I was accustomed to. I also did not have the appropriate experience and training for some of it. Though I love a good challenge, I failed miserably at this job. The experience could have made me risk averse; instead, it made me question my decisions and next steps. It made me reassess my goals and aspirations, and I made a decision that was far riskier than I had anticipated. I went from being slightly risk-averse to being a risk-taker, taking a break to write my book. I had the material I had researched and studied during my trip to the Himalayas and it was time to start putting them on paper. In hindsight, the failure was a great lesson to learn but it took me a couple of years of hard work to deal with the repercussions of my decision to take a break from my career and freelance as a writer and consultant. Leading a writer's life came with its own set of challenges and I learned to cope with them.

What if you fell off a tree and broke your leg and felt like a failure in front of your friends who are excellent climbers. However, because you fell, two years later, you devised a shoe or gloves to help people climb easily. This invention helped those who are physically challenged, and you won an award, and made lots of money. Would you care that you had fallen off the tree and hurt yourself couple of year ago? You see where I am going with this? Unfortunately, it is usually in hindsight that we recognize the reasons and objectives. One can however have faith that everything is a learning experience.

Easier said than done. Let's look at how to tackle our unnatural fears. Make a list of your internal and external fears. Remember some fears are positive and are nature's way of protecting us. I am talking about unnatural fears here. Do not be disheartened if you have a long list. The longer the list, the greater the opportunity to feel accomplished. If you are unable to make a list, then think back to all the times that you have felt anxiety or been in a depressed mood. They were probably caused by an underlying fear. Here is an example of how I identified one of my fears from an episode of anxiety.

Tool #1: Identifying underlying fears
Ask yourself:

Why am I anxious?

A: I just am.

What exactly am I feeling? Am I stressed? Am I anxious that I cannot cope?

A: I am stressed. I feel like I can't manage the project with everything that is going on. Too many moving parts.

Okay, we are getting somewhere now. Why do I feel I can't manage it when I have managed larger projects of work before?

A: I don't understand the technology. I can't understand what they're talking about in meetings.

Am I supposed to know everything?

A: No.

Then why am I panicking?

A: I don't know. I just am.

Can't I spend a weekend and go through the technology at a high level to understand it?

A: Yes, I could, but I need a break over the weekends. And even if I work through the weekend, there is no guarantee that I can manage this project.

What happens if I can't cope?

A: I fail. The project fails. I can't do that to myself.

What do you think are the core fears underlying my anxiety?

Fear of failure

Fear of damaging my reputation

Once you have determined your underlying fear, use the 'Disconnect' technique below.

Technique #8: Disconnect
Close your eyes and say, "Disconnect my energy from <name/s of the person/s, projects, clients, events or situations>"

Then say, "Disconnect any negative energy of <name/s of person/s, projects, clients, events or situations> from me."

And finally say, "Disconnect at all three levels of physical, mental, and emotional energy."

Say the above out loud if you need to.

Do it often and use it to disconnect from people, situations and events that are causing you anxiety. Disconnecting from someone you love does not mean you don't love or care for them. It simply allows you to stop your emotions from draining you so that you can function. If there is truly a conflict, you'll need to resolve it, but there is no point thinking about it twenty-four hours of the day, is there?

You can also use writing (as suggested in 'Technique #6'). At times, I write about my past failures and how I recovered from them, how much I learned from them. How they helped me grow and get me closer to my goals. By the end of this writing exercise, I feel better. Sometimes, I have to do this once a day until I get to the point where I no longer feel queasy, tired, or anxious.

Here's another example of self-questioning to determine underlying fears:

Why am I anxious?

A: It's my pitch presentation. What if doesn't go well?

Why do I think that?

A: Because yesterday during practice, it seemed like I couldn't articulate my value proposition.

Did I practice it on anyone? Did anyone give me any feedback?

A: No, but it felt that way to me.

Did I make any updates to it? Did I practice?

A: Yes.

So, my comment above is a self-assessment?

A: Maybe… yes.

Have I ever been wrong with self-assessments?

A: Yes, but I don't care. I'm nervous about it and I need this job.

So, I'm afraid of not getting the job.
A: Yes, of course and…
And…what is the other part?
A: I don't know. I mean… I haven't done this in a while now. Just makes me queasy.
What happens if I don't get it?
A: Don't say that. You're supposed to help me get it.
What happens if I don't get it?
A: I'll be upset. Maybe I should just go back to what I was doing.

What do you think my fears were?
- Fear of failure
- Fear of the impact of not getting the job on my confidence.

It is important to determine all our underlying fears, so you can work on them individually. Most likely, your self-assessments will lead to two to three core fears and if you work on them, you can take care of your anxieties and overarching negative emotions.

Here is an example of how I have helped a friend identify his underlying internal fear.

Why are you anxious about your relationship?
A: I want to get out of it. I don't want it. I don't want this anxiety.
Why don't you want it?
A: She doesn't cater to my needs. I want romance and love and I feel what we have is mundane.
Do you not feel love and romance in your relationship? Have you not had those experiences?
A: Yes, I have.
Can you recollect some experiences?
A: Yes.
Then why do you feel the way you do?
A: I don't know.
What exactly do you feel?

A: I don't trust what she says.
Why don't you trust her? Has she done anything to make you feel this way?
A: I don't know. I can't rely on what she says.
Have you spoken to her about this?
A: No.
Do you think she is generally honest?
A: Yes.
Then why do you think you can't trust her?
A: I don't know. I have been burned before and...

What do you think is the underlying fear is in the example above?
- Fear of trust being broken

It is easy to blame others for how we feel in a relationship, but it is important to understand that our own fears and insecurities make us anxious. In such situations, you can tell your partner how you feel and why you feel that way. If your partner genuinely loves you, he or she will make an effort to help you, but most often we must deal with our insecurities and fears ourselves.

Here are some questions to help you uncover typical anxieties and fears that pertain to love relationships.

Do you feel anxious when the other person goes cold on you suddenly?

Do you need to constantly seek comfort and assurance that the other person still loves you?

Is it possible that the other person has a genuine reason to need space or is busy with work or a personal challenge--but your anxiety causes you to feel insecure and behave in ways that are detrimental to the relationship?

Do you create negative stories in your mind that replay your past relationships until the situation turns out exactly like your past?

Do you get nervous when the other person does something that reminds you of your past? Do you instantly withdraw or erupt?

You may have uncovered some of these behaviors when you assessed your patterns in the chapter, 'Don't patent your patterns'. We shall now apply a method of breaking patterns suggested in the same chapter and build on it since fears too generally shows up as patterns.

Meditation #3: Advanced visualization and cognitive technique for fears.
Pre-meditation Work: Identify your underlying internal fears through self-assessment as suggested in 'Tool #1' above.

Think back to other times in the recent past when you may have had similar experiences caused by the same fear. Think back to your childhood when the fear may have taken root. Make a note of three events that were caused by your fear. Typical fears can be loneliness, rejection, abandonment, failure, betrayal and others.

Step 1: Get into a meditative state.

Sit on a chair with your feet flat on the floor and spine straight, shoulders relaxed. Hands on your knees with palms facing upward.

Visualize the energy of the Earth's core entering your feet and traveling through your legs to your hips and upper body. You may feel a pull on your feet.

Flush yourself with the core's energy.

Command it to suck out any negativity, negative entities, negative energies from your physical, mental, and emotional auras. It is also your connection to the planet that will keep you grounded throughout this meditation. It is important that we are grounded.

Step 2: Next, teleport yourself to the plane of abundance high above the Earth. The way teleportation works is, one moment you are seated on your chair and the next moment you are inside this energy plane. You do not visualize flying from one point to the other.

For those who are more visual, see this higher plane with light lemon-yellow energy laced with patches of light violet (based on my visuals of the energy planes). Feel weightless and float inside this energy plane. Bask in it. Absorb the energy through your crown chakra (on top of your head) and through your skin, into your muscles, bones and tissue. You may feel a tingling sensation on your head.

Allow yourself to absorb the abundance of joy, peace, health, wealth, success, and love.

Step 3: Remain inside this energy plane of abundance. Visualize feeling calm, joyful and centered, undeterred by anything or anyone.

Bring up the first fear event in front of you, as if you are watching it on a screen. Watch the event that caused you anxiety or whatever negative emotion you are dealing with. If it wasn't a conversation, simply visualize the series of activities that triggered the negative emotion. If the event is too traumatic to re-experience, visualize the person/s who caused you the negative emotions standing in front of you. Do not recreate the event.

See yourself undeterred and unafraid by the event, any conversations, revelations or presence. Smile and remain calm as you watch. You are no longer afraid, because you have fully detached from it. Take deep breaths. You can remain there as long as you want, feeling strong, calm, peaceful, and centered. Joyous that you have found your strength, calm and peace within. When you are ready, walk away -- toward an open doorway filled with bright sparkling lemon-yellow light, laced with violet colour – the energy of abundance. You enter the doorway and experience the infinite abundance of courage, love, peace, joy, calm, health, and wealth.

Repeat this step for the other two events. At the end of the third event, remain inside the doorway of abundance. Stay there as long as you like. Feel the joy and peace of healing yourself of your fear. Thank the energy planes and healing guides for enabling your healing. When you are ready, teleport yourself back to your chair. And feel the calm, peace, and joy settled inside you.

Next time you are in a similar real-life situation that causes fear or the emotional pattern you chose to break, see how you react. It can sometimes take one to two days to notice the impact of the above exercise, depending on the depth of the trauma and the trapped emotions you need to release. Some may feel bouts of emotions for a couple of days and if you do, release them. It is part of the healing process for you.

A Superhero understands that he or she has fears and is willing to tackle them and move forward. A Superhero knows the distinction between natural and unnatural fears. Allow the Universe to guide you to face and overcome your fears.

5 DEALING WITH EMOTIONS

This new AI chip is making me ...feel.
I don't even know what this feeling is called...

The Jolly Wally Therapy

A Jolly Wally stood outside an emotional care hospital with two distinct and separate sections. One was labeled 'EMOTIONAL' and the other 'OBJECTIVE.

To his surprise, those who emerged from the emotional section looked relieved while those who came from the objective section looked disappointed, upset, and angry. In his mind, he thought it should have been the other way around, but he continued on and walked up to the reception area.

"Which ward?" asked a calm but stern old Jolly Wally nurse.

"Could you help me understand why the ones from the objective ward seem more emotional than the ones from the emotional ward?" said the Jolly Wally.

"Which ward?" she repeated. "You're holding up the line."

"I'll take the emotional ward, thank you," he said, hoping that he too would look relieved when he left the hospital.

Hesitant and unsure, he entered the 'EMOTIONAL' ward. There were several rooms, each with a plaque on its door. One read 'anger,' another read, 'grief,' yet another read, 'pregnancy frustrations (open to both sexes).' The corridor was long with rooms dedicated to all kinds of emotions. The Jolly Wally knocked on a door for 'anger' and was ushered into a room full of not-so-jolly Wallys. When it was his turn to see the doctor, he asked the same question that he had asked the nurse at the entrance. The doctor smiled and slapped him across his face.

"What did you do that for?"

The doctor slapped him again. The Wally grabbed the doctor's arm.

"You recognize that you are angry?" said the doctor calmly.

"Are you kidding?"

"Well, you recognize that you are angry and you know why you are angry."

"This is ridiculous therapy," said the Wally and stood up.

"Wait, it just started," said the doctor but the Jolly Wally left in a hurry.

As he walked out of the door, he realized why everyone looked relieved to be leaving the EMOTIONAL ward. He wondered why the ones from the OBJECTIVE ward were angry and emotional. He decided he was not going to find out.

SUPER-ME

***

Like many of you, I have had emotions of failure, in sports and academics caused by my expectations of myself and others' expectations of me. I remember wanting to get a distinction as an undergraduate only to make my parents proud. All through school and college, I studied because I wanted my parents to be proud of me. I did it also because I thought they expected it of me. I have felt rejection from friends in the past, caused by my unrealistic expectations of them. I remember missing some of my friends who had moved away, especially the ones I had grown close to. At times, the feeling of rejection in my childhood also rose from being teased and I remember retaliating by teasing others. As I got older, the failures and feelings of rejection had a greater impact on my behavior. The fear of failure caused anxiety, stress and unnecessary worry. The fear of rejection caused me to be over-adapting, understanding, and accepting of bad behaviors from others.

About 80 percent of all our negative emotions are caused by thoughts that are connected in one way or another to,

1) our attachments and,
2) expectations of ourselves and others.

These attachments may be with people or with outcomes we are trying to achieve. Much of our unhappiness is self-inflicted, caused by our own fears and insecurities. Our fears and insecurities can create stories in our minds, which then cause emotional ups and downs. If we act upon them, then we can create more challenges by how we react to these emotions. If you are stressed and anxious, lose patience, and snap and shout at others, then you are creating more negative energy and negative karma for yourself.

A note of clarification: Letting go of attachments and expectations does not mean you become unemotional or lacking in compassion. It does not mean you don't love people; it simply means that you cut through your expectations of them. Lower the expectations, lessen the pressures on the other person--as long as you are not letting the other person take you for granted, be abusive in some way, or walk over your value system. For any relationship to work, be it love or friendships, the value system of both parties must be aligned. If not, the relationship will have troubles. I am referring to expectations we have of our friends, partners, colleagues, and subordinates--and what we believe are their expectations of us.

While emotions are necessary for me to understand myself, I'm mindful not to remain inside my head and keep analyzing them. I do reserve some time in the day for this analysis but the rest of the time, I try remain objective and focus on my work at hand, the actions I must take, and the people I must help. I confess that I have been in situations where I have spent an entire day thinking about an incident. The thoughts build up more stories in my head and it does not help that I'm also a fiction writer. The stories have twists and turns and underlying meanings that only I can decipher. At the end of the day I am exhausted, not from physical activities but from thoughts and emotions working through my head. In such situations, you can break the thought. Go for a run or a walk or some kind of physical exercise. Clean your room! Give your brain a break.

How often have you made assumptions about a certain person or situation based on your past experiences, and how often have these assumptions been wrong? How often have you behaved a certain way only to find out that the other person did not mean what you thought they meant? This happens all the time between people we love, people we work with. Different people behave and act differently under emotional stress, so it is best to be mindful of assumptions we make about one another and our behaviors. Our mind is a beautiful tool given to us to use when we need it. The monkey mind (addicted to thinking all the time) is not what must govern us. Thich Nhat Hanh and Eckhart Tolle provide some profound explanations about this in their books. This is where the concept of mindfulness comes in.

Here are four techniques to help you deal with emotions. Try them and see what works for you. I have successfully tried each of the four techniques and use them at different times.

For example, if I'm in a hurry, I go for Technique #10 and Technique #11, which are quick and easy ways to disconnect. I may use Technique #9 or Technique #12 when I have some spare time. I have also used a mix of techniques. For example, Technique #10 works well with Technique #11 or Technique #12.

Technique #9: A-B-C-D of E-(motions)
This tool relies on the power of the mind.

Step A: Accept that you are feeling the emotion.

Step B: Breathe it out. Pause your mind and take a few deep breaths. With every breath, exhale your emotions.

I take deep breaths and open my heart energy gateway (positioned over the heart). If need be, you can touch your chest and say in your mind or out loud, "Activate my heart gateway but shield it from any negative energy around me."

Step C: Convince yourself that the Universe is looking after you. That it will always do what is best for you.

Tell yourself, *"It is not the end of the world."* Keep telling yourself that. Say it out loud if you need to. Keep reminding yourself of that. Use some of the statements mentioned in the earlier chapters.

Use writing as therapy as mentioned earlier or use autosuggestion if you are not a writing person.

Step D: Distract yourself with something funny or an exercise – physical or mental, whichever works for you. I find cleaning your clutter is a great way of mindful distraction. Clearing your space helps clear your mind.

Do things that make you feel better. I write because it brings me joy.

A friend of mine likes to read stories about creative people who have struggled in their lives and then made it big. As a writer, I can certainly appreciate such stories. Another friend believes in aromatherapy and uses drops of Bergamot and Clary Sage. She rubs them on her palms and then takes deep breaths. I have tried it and it did make me feel more relaxed, perhaps the smell distracted my mind. My mother prefers to pray and that brings her peace and calm. Yet another friend goes for a run or a swim in the ocean. You may not feel like following any of the pointers above. If not, ask a friend to force you to engage in an activity (preferably physical), that you typically enjoy or simply go for a long walk in the woods or garden.

You cannot try the **A-B-C-D** of **E** once and master it. You will need to practice it each time you have a challenging emotion, be it anxiety, fear, grief, or anger.

Technique #10: Breathe out and disconnect
This is a combination of Technique #4 and Technique #8 from previous chapters. It relies on concepts of energy sciences, one of them being that energy follows thought. As you think, so you will be.

Step 1: Acknowledge the emotion.

Step 2: Breathe out the emotion. Pause your mind and thoughts and breathe out your feelings and emotions. An easy way to do this is to say to yourself that you are breathing out the emotion as you physically breathe. Take three to five deep breaths to allow yourself to calm.

Step 3: Next, disconnect from situations and people who are causing you the emotion through a set of three statements. Your energy will follow your thought and intention. Close your eyes and say, *"Disconnect from <name/s of the person/s, clients, events or situations>"*

Then say, *Disconnect at all three levels: physical, mental and emotional."*

Say the above three statements out loud if you need to. This might sound a bit silly at first, but energy follows thoughts and intention. If you are reading this book, I hope you keep an open mind to trying these exercises. See how you feel.

Depending upon how intense the situation is, you may need to practice this disconnecting technique a few times during the day. Each time you find yourself thinking about the event, try this combination technique. I use it all the time for all kinds of emotional challenges. I also like to do it before I begin any kind of meditation. I would recommend you try it with your meditations.

Technique #11: Mindfulness seeds.
This technique is similar to Technique #5 but has a variation using concepts presented by Thich Naht Hahn. The philosophy behind it is that all of us have seeds of positive and negative emotions inside us. These seeds open when we are triggered by events. We have the ability to command negative emotions to return to seed form and instead bring positive emotions out of their seeds to flourish.

Step 1: Accept that you are going through the emotion.

Step 2: Pause your thoughts and breathe deeply. I tend to continue breathing until my racing mind has calmed.
I don't fight my thoughts but breathe them out, disconnect from them, and calm my mind.

Step 3: In this step, I command my negative emotion to return to its seed form inside me. Then, I invoke the opposite seeds of positive emotions to take over.

Meditation #4: Extended visualization for stress release
This meditation is available at www.beyoursuperhero.org.
  Remember: Energy follows thought
  Duration: 14 minutes
  When to use this meditation: To replenish your positive energy, to heal yourself of physical, mental or emotional pain or negativities

Preferred Time: Early morning after a bath or shower
Preferred location: Anywhere quiet

Step 1: Getting into the zone... Sit on a chair with your feet flat on the floor and spine straight. Your palms on your knees face upward. Close your eyes and take a few deep breaths. Release any tension you have in your body. Any pain, physical, emotional or mental, any stress, grief, anxiety, fears, and all negativities and negative energies.

If your mind is distracted at any point during this meditation, calmly bring it back to focus on your breath. You can also say, *"Disconnect from that thought."* Feel your body relax into your posture. Relax your shoulders Relax your head and your neck. Take a few deep breaths. And keep breathing out any negative energies inside you.

Step 2: Disconnect from Negativities... Now say in your mind,
"Disconnect from other people (you may say the names of specific people if there are any), negative entities, negative energies, events and situations"

Then say, *"Disconnect at all three levels of physical, mental, and emotional"*

Take deep breaths and feel light as the negative connections disconnect from you.

Step 3: Align with the Earth... Ground yourself... You may bring your hands together in front of your chest like a Namaskar salutation – bring both your hands together, palms and fingers touching each other, pointing upwards, in front of your chest and bow your head gently.

Say in your mind, *"I am grateful to our planet for giving me everything I need. I salute our planet and align with its energy."*

You may continue to keep your hands in the Namaskar salutation or place them on your knees with your palms facing upward. Now feel the Earth's energy enter through your feet and rise to your legs and the rest of your body. You may feel a tingling sensation or a strong pull on your feet.

If you are a visual person, visualize this energy entering through your feet and spreading inside every part of your body. Breathe deeply. Allow this energy to open your chakras. Remain in this position until the Earth's energy has filled your body and energized your chakras.

Step 4: Connect with the healing energies… Visualize yourself in the higher planes of the Universe. You are surrounded by sparkling light lemon-yellow light interlaced with patches of light violet color. Smile as you feel the sparkling white light penetrate through your skin and fill your body. Breathe deeply and see the energy fill your body, your palms, your arms, shoulders, neck, head, chest, your back, stomach, hips, legs, feet. Breathe in the positive energy.

Then say, *"I command the energy to heal my physical pain (if you have any). I command the energy to heal my negative emotions and thoughts. Disintegrate any negative thoughts, negative emotions, negative entities, negative energies inside me and replace them with positive energy."*

Breathe and allow the healing to take place. Bask in this positivity and remain in the higher planes for as long as you like. Feel the peace and calm within you.

Step 5: Shield yourself… Take a few deep breaths and visualize a protective transparent shield around you, at all three levels: physical, mental, and emotional.

Then say, *"I command my shield to protect me from any negative energies, entities, negative people, situations, events. I command my shield to only allow positive energy to enter."*

Now take a deep breath and visualize your protective shield around you. Then return to where you are seated and feel the strong connection from your feet to the planet.

Slowly open your eyes and SMILE!!

I have also used my experiences with the meditations in this book to elevate myself to higher planes when I have felt lower emotions. For example, if I'm feeling sad due to an event or challenge, I simply close my eyes, connect to the Earth's core and then visualize teleporting myself to higher planes. I do not need to go through each step in the meditations. However, this is only possible when you have been practicing these meditations with all steps for some time. The more you practice, the faster you can break through the clutter in your mind and move to higher planes. The more you practice, the easier it becomes to gain clarity.

When I follow the two steps above, my negative emotions dissipate instantly. They are replaced by my intention of peace and calm. I remain in the higher plane for a few seconds before returning. While the higher planes help us feel calm and peaceful, it is important to maintain your connection with the Earth. Hence, the connection to the planet is the first step.

Technique #12: Advanced technique.
A more advanced technique that is available to seasoned meditators and healers is to connect with one's subconscious mind. Those who are not regular practitioners can give it a go to see how it works for them.

When you are going through a negative experience or emotion, pause and with intention suggest to yourself, *"Connect with my subconscious mind"*. Take a deep breath. For advanced practitioners, you may feel a release instantly through a yawn or feeling of lightness. And you will notice how the emotions caused by the conscious mind dissipates. Remain connected with the subconscious mind until you feel calm and aligned. Then return to whatever you were doing.

Regardless of the technique you choose, it's important to practice mindfulness every day. Have you noticed how our minds constantly wander and cause thoughts that create emotions and dramas inside us? Have you noticed how our minds cannot stand still and are addicted to thinking? So how does one train one's mind? Through yoga and meditation. By doing activities that take your mind off thinking. These may include sports, physical labour, music, dance, art forms, and nature walks with reliance on our four senses of touch, smell, sound, sight.

Experiencing an emotion helps us understand our underlying fears and insecurities but how we react to the emotion can affect our karmas. If we get anxious and shout at people, we are allowing the emotion to create more negative karma with those we are shouting at. Instead, if we accept the anxiety and allow it to pass--then we have mastered how to learn from our emotions.

Just as we must be patient with our lessons, we must be also be patient with our emotions. Some emotions may take longer to pass. While emotions are our gateway to understanding our underlying fears, it is not necessary to always assess the underlying fear or cause. At times, we may simply need to acknowledge the emotion and let it pass. Over-analysis is as bad as the conscious monkey mind itself that is addicted to thinking. You end up trying to replace one bad habit with another bad habit. Instead, a healthy balance of introspection and action is important. Some days, you may go without introspection and only focus on action. Reach out to your subconscious and align with it through meditation. Allow it to help you.

Emotions related to depressed moods are tougher to deal with. You may have good days and not so good days. I make sure I get ample sun and vitamin D. I force myself to go to the gym or play a sport as often as I can. Walk! I find walking in a park is one of the best exercises for me. Find yours. I watch movies that are light and entertaining. I watch stand-up comics online or at a club and I write because writing brings me joy. Some people need external help. Do not hesitate to reach out. The Universe provides us with tools, whether these tools are within us or in the form of advice from others. It is up to us to be open to them. When all else fails, I close my eyes and ask the Universe to help me. Ask and it will always provide. But be ready to accept help when it arrives. It won't always will it come to you in the form you prefer or expect. A Superhero know this and is open to advice, even when it is not in the form or format of his or her preference.

6 KARMA IS ... WHAT!?

SUPER-ME

The Jolly Wally Woodcutter's Irony

Before the woodcutter in Chapter 2 collapsed on the enchanted grass, he had been busy cutting down a tree in his garden. The genie had appeared and suggested that he stop.

"You forgot to ask for a long life," she said with a sigh.

The woodcutter stood with his axe in hand and felt his legs tremble.

"You don't mean...?" he stuttered.

The genie nodded and said, "Sorry."

The woodcutter's head felt heavy and then everything around him went dark.

The genie sighed again and was about to leave when the tree the woodcutter had been cutting, cracked... and fell on her...

Karma is... what?

***

Simply stated, karma is a term used to collectively represent what you think, what you speak, and what you do in action. If you have a positive impact on a person, then from that person's perspective you have created good karma. Unknowingly, at times, we can create negative karma through negative thoughts and negative speech about people. We take actions not knowing that they will cause pain to others. When this happens, it's best to refrain from self-guilt, and instead use the situation to be more self-aware in future. Consciously tell yourself to remember the situation and not repeat it.

Have you met people who are constantly complaining and negative about others? Their speech and thoughts exude negativity. They tend to attract other negative people and form gossip circles. These people also sap other people's energy. Have you ever met someone and felt drained immediately? Or felt it after having a conversation with them? Have you met people who take pleasure in putting others down? They thrive on the lower emotions of anger, fear, and anxiety, and suck out your energy in the process. Be aware of such people.

You have probably also met people who have very positive energy. All of us love to be around such people, and we can feel when it's genuine. If someone tries to fake being positive, people will eventually see through it. We are sensitive to energies around us. Each one of us. Some use the term energy while others personify the energy as feelings, behaviors, traits, and types of people. When I'm among people who talk negatively about an event or other people, it starts to bring me down. I try and break up the negative talk, but after a while, if they continue, I leave and surround myself with more positive people, and nature. You can never go wrong with nature and its beauty.

Negative people are everywhere because it is easier for us to be negative than positive. Being negative means you blame others or external circumstances for your challenges. You don't accept ownership or responsibility for your situation. Gossiping and putting someone down makes you feel superior. Negative people, rich or poor, educated or not, sophisticated or not, are generally pessimistic. I have come across people who have attained great levels of success, fame, and wealth but continue to be negative. You may wonder how they were able to attain such success. They may have used their willpower, discipline, and charm to achieve results. They probably also have good karma from the past that has provided them with gifts. Karma is not the only factor for success; neither is positivity by itself. But positivity does bring us joy, peace, and clarity in addition to access to abundance—if we pull additional levers like willpower, discipline, perseverance, etc. – necessary elements of success. People who are successful but negative often suffer from insecurities, fears, and dissatisfactions and are not at peace with themselves. Some are also depressed or have other mental health challenges. Some are lonely because no one wants to associate with them. And they believe it is because everyone is jealous of them. While that might be true in some cases, more often, people do not associate with a negative person because of his or her attitude.

Those who have learned to be positive and create positive karma are able to be happy, satisfied, and feel joy within, irrespective of their social or economic status. Why not aim to be successful, famous, wealthy, and positive? Wouldn't that be the best way? If you had all the wealth and fame you wanted, wouldn't you want to change your thought process and align with being more positive toward others? Create more positive karma for this lifetime and the next (if you believe in rebirth). It is not a surprise that many old scripts and philosophies (western and eastern) talk about refraining from criticism and badmouthing others and recommend that we focus on positives in people and situations. The framework of Karma is a framework that can help us understand why we go through certain conflicts or challenges.

Karma can be categorized as:
1. Self-karma – your actions, thoughts, and speech. If you meet someone and think badly of them, yet smile and wish them well, you are creating negative karma. While it is a good habit to wish people well and acknowledge their presence, a better habit is to think positively about people. Energy follows thought. If you think negatively, you are creating negative karma or energy.

2. Family or lineage-based karma – your family's actions, thoughts and speech. We are all affected by the energy of our family members, by the lessons and teachings that we call our upbringing.

My father is an impatient man and my mother tries to be patient. At times, when we see through her impatience, she blames my father for it. He does tend to push all her wrong buttons. You see, patience and a sense of personal space are not part of my paternal vocabulary. For instance, if I said I will be home by 7:00 p.m. and it is 6:55 p.m., I'll receive a phone call from my father asking me where I am. If the clock were to strike 8:00 p.m., I would have received at least two missed calls, one from him and one from my mother, who was probably coaxed into calling me. Any later than two hours, and my father would have driven my mother to the brink of an anxiety attack. Knowing this, all I have to do is make a quick call and tell them that I will be late. While parents are biologically programmed to worry about their children, the concern in this context is how much and under what circumstances. In this example, the anxiety is unnecessary. This trait of impatience and anxiety has surfaced in my life too and I have mindfully accepted it and then dealt with it, using the tools in this book.

My father may be impatient and anxious, but he also has some rare positive traits. He is, for example, not only never jealous of anyone, but is genuinely happy at other people's successes and joys. He makes it his joy. He is also most compassionate toward anyone who has been through a failure. He understands failure since he's been through many and is always there to encourage people. He understands what it is like to be teased and is compassionate toward those who are bullied.

Writing has played a big role in making me patient. The process of getting published has certainly upped this ability. Trying to give up my sugar addiction has taken my patience to a whole new level, especially, since I am someone who can eat cream and donuts for breakfast, lunch, and dinner.

There have been times when I've been angry at my parents for events in my childhood. Situations where I thought my parents could have done things differently and that could have changed some of my traits and behaviors. While it is easy to blame them for my challenges, I believe these events made me learn and grow. If I hadn't experienced an event that caused me guilt and shame, I would have never been able to understand what it feels like to go through it. And be able to help other people. If I hadn't experienced guilt, I would have never have learned to accept myself. I would not be able to understand my mentees who are challenged with acceptance. So, should I blame my parents for how they managed conflicts and situations (to the best of their ability)? Or should I make peace my past and keep in mind how it taught me lessons, so I could become my own Superhero? It is pointless to play the blame game for what happened in the past; instead, learn from your experiences and emotions and heal yourself. This acceptance is not of the events but of the lessons you have learned from them. The acceptance is of the growth you have experienced.

Do I think I needed to go through traumatic events in my childhood? I don't, but I acknowledge that they have shaped me and have helped me grow spiritually and emotionally. Would I have preferred to learn my lessons and grow without the traumas? Absolutely. Would I have preferred that the lesson come to me in milder doses? That would be more palatable, I reckon. But I've made peace with it because I see the significant growth it has brought in me.

3. Associative karma – cumulative karma of groups you belong to, the karma of the company you keep, karma of the city you live in, karma of the country.

The karma of people living in a city creates the energy for the city, and this energy affects everyone who lives there or visits. Similarly, the karma of people in a country affects the energy in the country. If we look at how social media affects us, you can see a clear experiment of associative karma. When you spend time with someone who is always depressed, you will start to feel it yourself. If you spend time with someone who is always happy and excited, you will feel this excitement. It is the transfer of energy or or karma (thought ~ energy, action ~ energy, speech ~ energy).

Have you ever visited a country and experienced the energy of the place? Come to New York and make a trip to Time Square at midnight and you will see what I mean. Or go to Queenstown in the South Island of New Zealand and you will experience a very different kind of energy from NYC. Some call it, vibe, some, energy. The people, and even the animals and trees contribute to the energy of a place. This is associative karma.

Similarly, when you are in a group of positive minded people, you will feel the positivity. When you mingle with negative people, you will feel the negativity. This is also associative karma.

4. Past life karma – Eastern philosophies believe in reincarnation of the soul and this gives rise to the concept of past life karma.

Positive karma comes back to us in the form of help during tough situations: Doors open for us when we least expect it. Negative karma comes back to us in the form of tough situations and causes emotional, mental and, in some cases, physical pain. Not all difficult situations are due to karma. Remember, many of our lessons relate to goals we have set for ourselves.

Irrespective of the type of karma, the experiences and lessons they drive lead us toward our growth. So ultimately, all karma leads to positive outcomes.

For example, if you face illness or adversity, and this makes you more compassionate toward others or helps you grow spiritually, then what seemed negative led to a positive outcome. If you are able to think of your life as a journey, then you will be able to accept this thought. Many of us get so bogged down by the emotions of challenging situations that we are unable to look ahead. It is natural and normal to have emotions. They are a way for our spirit and body to communicate with us. If you can understand and interpret your emotions, you will be able to master them and align yourself with your purpose. This understanding and interpretation comes with introspection and in some cases, with help from external coaches. Never try to stifle your emotions. They will only accumulate and lead to a disease or other ailment.

I believe that the Universe is constantly seeking to create situations to help us neutralize our negative karmas and achieve the best in our lives. Sometimes these situations come in the form of challenges or conflicts; at other times they are positive events. I like to think of challenges as problems that I need to solve. If you take a problem-solving approach and instead of casting blame, problems will be easier to tackle. The Universe' goal is to give us everything we want and need but it is up to us to recognize this truth and to align with it, so we can reap the rewards. Those who have learned this, and have aligned themselves, have gained access to abundance.

Alignment with the Universe also requires an understanding of how it operates, how we are connected to it, self-awareness, and tried and tested techniques. This book aims to give you all of the above.

7 NO ESCAPE

Irony of Human Conflicts

In Search of Happiness

A wealthy Jolly Wally woman decided that she was not happy in her relationship of many years. She broke up with her partner, traveled far and wide, and eventually arrived at the door of a wise old Jolly Wally.

"What is it you seek? It looks like you have everything you need," said the wise one, noticing her exquisite taste in clothes.

"I want to find happiness," said our Jolly Wally. "You are a wise one. Can you show me the path to happiness?"

The wise one nodded and ushered her to a small dark room next to his cowshed.

"Make yourself at home here," he said to her.

That night, the Jolly Wally woman tried to sleep but dung flies buzzed around her all night and kept her awake. The stench of cow dung stuck deep inside her nose. She did not complain. The following night, she was able to sleep, only because she was too tired to stay awake. But just as the sun rose, she was awakened by the wretched rooster outside her room. Days passed with many sleepless nights and one morning she burst into tears.

"I can't do this anymore! I came here to find happiness but all you have shown me is a bunch of cow shit. And now I'm sad and..."

"If you don't feel sadness, how will you appreciate happiness when you find it?"

"But I appreciate happiness already. That's why I've been looking for it. I am done here."

The old Wally wished her well and she returned to her father's home. The bed was warm and cozy; no buzzing flies or roosters around. She slept all night and all day and when she awoke the next morning, breakfast was served in bed.

"It is true what they say," she thought, "Home is where happiness lies."

But days passed, and she was back to feeling restless again. Perhaps if she found herself a partner, she would be happy, she thought. The Universe heard her and she met someone wonderful who shared her quest for happiness, her zest for life, and her interest in business matters. They chatted and laughed, they joked and cried with laughter. Our Jolly Wally had found her match. But soon after they met, her new partner decided it was time to leave, to go in search for happiness.

SUPER-ME

"But aren't you happy with me here?" she said.

Her pleas fell on deaf ears. She cried that day and realized what her ex-partner may have experienced when she had herself left in pursuit of happiness. Mustering courage, she visited her ex-partner.

"I'm sorry I left," she said. "But I'm back now. Do you think we could try and be together again?"

Her ex-partner took a deep breath and nodded. "On my terms...."

Our Jolly Wally agreed to the terms and moved in but within the first week, she realized why she had left. Nothing had changed. The old emotions of dissatisfaction and restlessness returned. The feeling of being trapped returned.

"This was a big mistake," she announced. "I'm sorry but I must return to my parents and will probably never come back."

Saying this, she left but instead of going to her parents, she visited the wise old Wally again.

"You're back?" he said with a smile.

"I cannot find happiness anywhere," she said. "I've tried everything. Am I not deserving of it? Am I not a good person... a good..."

"Stop!... what you need is to find joy, not happiness."

"Why didn't you say so before? You sent me on this wild goose chase. What must I do? Can you help me find it?"

"Indeed!" said the old wise Wally. "Go wash the cows while I think about it."

She washed the cows, excitedly. They licked her arms to thank her and she giggled and laughed. When she was done, the wise one asked her to feed the beggars.

She fed them, and they blessed her in return. The more they blessed her, the more she fed them.

"Keep some food for others too," shouted the wise one. "Go help the children now. They can do with some lessons with you."

The Jolly Wally spent the rest of her day teaching the children. When the sun was about to set, she returned to the wise Wally.

"Thank you," she said calmly. "I have found my joy."

The old Wally nodded approvingly and wished her well. She returned home to help her father. Together, they did well and with her share of profits, she built a small school for poor children, a homeless shelter, and an animal care facility. All things that had brought her joy. She hadn't found a partner yet, but that is another story…

***

Pick your toughest challenge or event you've experienced in your life and think about how it has changed you, the way you think, or act today. What is the one thing you learned from it? Did the lesson help you grow emotionally? Mentally?

Now close your eyes and think about an event that caused you happiness. Did it lead to any growth within you? Emotional or mental? When we experience happiness, we don't grow. The path to get there may have involved conflicts and challenges that presented opportunities for growth. For example, if you won an award, you may have had to deal with acute competition, push yourself, and work harder than you ever had before. The effort required to win the award allowed you to learn and grow.

This chapter is dedicated to understanding our conflicts and challenges, regardless of who started them, who is innocent or who is to blame. Categorizing these lessons helps me understand better. When I'm able to understand, I'm able to resolve conflicts faster or make peace with difficult situations. I'm also aware that if I do not resolve conflicts and learn from them, similar conflicts will recur.

Unfortunately, we humans experience the highest growth when we go through our toughest conflicts and challenges. I wish there was a school we could go to learn our tough lessons. Schools can give us tools, just as this book aims to do, but it is our ability to use them that truly enables our emotional, mental, and spiritual growth. A conflict creates opportunity for us to be more creative and innovative. The conflict may be external, between two parties, or internal, inside our minds and connected to our values, ethics, and culture. Either way, if you take a problem-solving approach, you will get better results. Some may take more time to experience their emotions before they get to an objective state of assessment and problem solving.

I have grouped my own lessons from conflicts and challenges into three categories. I hope they give you a sense of how to categorize your own challenges and conflicts and the lessons they drive.

Lessons related to my goals or aspirations. All of these lessons are related to my aspirations of being a writer and coach.

- Learning to be patient
- Learning to deal with my emotions
- Learning to be more objective in decision making
- Learning to be more compassionate
- Learning to rely on the universe and allow it to do its magic

Lessons related to karma
- Dealing with trust issues in relationships
- Dealing with acceptance of myself and others
- Dealing with anger

Lessons related to patterns
- Learning to be patient
- Learning to deal with my emotions
- Dealing with trust issues in relationships
- Dealing with acceptance of myself and others

Notice how some lessons go across categories. Specifically, the last category of patterns will likely include lessons from the other two categories.

Category 1: Lessons related to our aspirations.
Lessons in this category were discussed in great detail in the first few chapters. To be able to write my book, I needed to learn to deal with my anxieties, so I could patiently write and edit chapters. I needed to deal with my depression and emotions in order to write with conviction. I needed to find my true purpose and value system, so I could suggest it in the

book. I learned to rely on the Universe and let go of trying to control outcomes. All of these lessons were related to my aspirations and goals. One might argue that all lessons we learn are connected to our goals. Yes, that is likely but there are some lessons related to our karma.

Category 2: Lessons related to karma

A few years ago, I ended a relationship that took me considerable time to get over. Then one day I met someone and decided to date again. This relationship too had its challenges. However, my current partner reminded me of myself in my last relationship and I found myself in my ex-partner's shoes. I got a sense of what my ex-partner might have been through while we were together. It made me realize that I had made many mistakes, misunderstood my ex-partner many times, and in the process caused hurt. The challenges I faced in my new relationship taught me lessons of self-realization. They were related to the karma I created in my previous relationship; I had to go through the same experience that I put my ex-partner through. Ultimately, this lesson may help me with my aspirations of being in a loving and giving relationship. However, it is distinctly karmic.

The easiest way to determine whether a lesson is related to karma is to rely on your thoughts, and intuition. Our subconscious minds have excellent memories, not only of pain and misery we have experienced but also of any harm—mental, physical, or emotional—that we may have caused others. Some of us are more intuitive than others and can sense when our behaviors or actions cause negative emotions. Women in particular are more sensitive, with an innate sense not only about themselves but also others.

If a challenge reminds you of an instance where you may have put another person through a similar emotion or challenge, then it is a clear sign of a karmic lesson. Not everyone's conscience kicks in. I have dealt with individuals who may have been clinical psychopaths or may have had extreme forms of selfishness where they only see their challenges and are oblivious to how they cause hurt to others. For some, it may be a defense mechanism based on hurt experienced in their childhood. Irrespective of what and who they are, karmic lessons do come back to us. They may not be the exact situation or circumstance but the emotions they drive will be similar to the ones you caused others.

Category 3: Lessons related to patterns

Both categories of lessons (goal-related or karmic) can show up as patterns – the third category. If karmic, then the pattern continues until we have neutralized our karma (realized our negative actions toward others and made amends or changes in ourselves). If related to our goals, then the pattern continues until we have acquired a skill or trait we need to attain our goals. This third category is an extension of the first two. When the first category repeats, it becomes a pattern related to our aspirations and goals. When the second category repeats, it becomes a pattern related to our karma. Some may be happy to limit the categorization to the first two.

When I know a certain lesson is related to my goals and aspirations, I spend time understanding the lesson it is driving and take concerted effort to learn it. During one of my volunteering opportunities, within the first couple of weeks I got a sense that I did not fit into the culture of the organization. I kept telling myself that I was being impatient and not giving it my best shot. I motivated myself and did everything I needed to achieve success in my role. I stayed on. Six months later, I made a list of reasons for enjoying my role and reasons for not liking it. The latter was longer than the former, but I stuck it out, telling myself that I needed to be patient and I needed to allow myself the time to be sure. By end of the first year, I started experiencing difficult situations that triggered negative emotions like frustration, anger, and a feeling of restlessness and anxiety. I assessed these situations and decided that they were meant to teach me to be more patient. I allowed the emotions to pass but they returned every week like a reminder. I quit. Two years later, I bumped into someone I had worked with at the organization and she mentioned how things had changed since I left. I decided to volunteer for them again and started working for the same team. Within a week, I had to deal with situations and challenges that reminded me of why I had left the first time. This is an example of a pattern. We face such patterns everyday with friends, with family, with our partners too. In this instance, the pattern made me realize that I needed to be more compassionate and patient with the people I worked with. The ability of compassion and patience would also help me coach different types of people and youth in particular.

Have you ever gone back to a past relationship, only to realize that nothing has changed? That no matter how much you try and remedy it, you go through the exact same experiences and emotions – the very reasons you left the relationship in the first place? Usually, such lessons are related to karma. It may be my karma with the person -- which brings me to another element based on Eastern beliefs – past life karma. Sometimes, we go through difficult situations to neutralize our past life negative karmas with specific individuals. It means we had "business" with a particular soul in a past life and we are still working it out in this lifetime. But to subscribe to that line of thought, one must believe in the concept of reincarnation. It is a tough one for those who have not been brought up with Eastern philosophy. You may not believe in past lives and reincarnation, but as long as you're able to find a positive outcome or lesson to be learned from your challenges and conflicts, you will get through them faster and move on.

The concept of karma is also meant to help us let go – for our own peace of mind. If I accept that I may have had a past life karma with someone who caused me much hurt, I am able to forgive the person and move on. Storing anger and hurt inside is more harmful for me. Why do that to yourself when you can use a mechanism to let go and move on to find your joy? If there are other methods to objectively move on without trapping these negative emotions within yourself, use them.

I once worked with someone who came across as being very set in her ways. Unaware of the boundaries she had created, I unwittingly crossed them. As weeks passed, I found her constantly pushing back against my ideas and thoughts. She had the best intentions for our project but I kept pushing the wrong buttons. Tension grew. I confronted her once and that helped a little. I tried to socialize with her and get to know her and that helped too but I could see that she had developed certain notions about me and my working style based on her past experiences with other people. She was also extremely autocratic in her approach. I thought she might come around with time, but she didn't. She was what we call a control freak. She was also happy to provide feedback to others but couldn't handle feedback herself. She was terrible at delegating.

So, what did I do to reduce conflict with her?

Meditation #5: Removing blockages with people
This meditation is a slight variation on the very first one in the book in chapter, 'Make a wish'.

Key: Energy follows thought and intention. If negative thoughts arise during this meditation, calmly disconnect from them.

Say in your mind, 'Disconnect from that thought' and then return to the meditation.

If you'd like to experience a guided meditation, please refer to an extended version of this meditation, available at www.beyoursuperhero.org.

Step 1: Sit on a chair with your feet flat on the floor, hands on your knees, palms facing upward and spine straight, shoulder relaxed. Be comfortable on the chair. You can also do this lying on your bed as long as you keep your spine straight.

Take a few deep breaths and settle into the chair.

Step 2: Visualize the energy from the Earth's core penetrating through your feet. Feel a pull on your feet as the energy enters and rises through your legs to the rest of your body. If you are a visual person, you may give this energy a color (I like to think of it as light sparkling green or the color of the molten core – a yellowish orange). See the energy move through your meridians, organs, muscles, bone and tissue to all parts of your body and your auras – physical, mental, and emotional.

Remember energy follows thoughts and intention.

Command the core's energy to destroy and remove all negative feelings, emotions, negativities, negative thoughts, anxieties, sadness, grief, anger, all lower negative emotions and feelings. Command the energy to destroy and remove any negative entities.

Take deep breaths and allow the core's energy to relieve you of all negativities.

Step 3: Teleport yourself to a higher energy plane of bright white sparkling healing light high above the Earth.

The way teleportation works is, one moment you're seated on your chair and the next moment you visualize yourself inside the positive healing energy plane where you feel weightless and float. When you look down from this energy plane, you can see the Earth as a small speck of light far away.

Bask in this higher energy.

With intention or thought, bless yourself with its energy.

Open the energy gateway on top of your head (crown chakra) and allow the energy to enter. You may feel a tingling sensation on your head as the energy mingles with the Earth's core inside you.

Command the energy to destroy and disintegrate all negativities, negative entities, negative energies inside you. Command it to circulate through your body and allow your body, skin, tissue, bones, and auras to absorb it.

Step 4: Thank the universe for helping you heal. Thank it for your life and for all the positive things you have received.

Thank those who have helped you in your life. People who have helped you with your school, your work, your relationships.

Thank your family and friends who love you.

Rely on your intuition to allow it to identify people to thank. You may see them as faces or names flashing in your mind.

Feel the gratitude within you. Smile.

Now bless the people who have caused you pain, in your personal life, relationships, ex-partners, ex-lovers, people who have treated you badly at work, caused you stress at work, anyone you are currently challenged with. You can bring these people up to the healing plane or you can simply send them blessings from the healing plane. with intention and thought.

This will help neutralize your negative karma with them and help you forgive them and move on. You do not need to keep in touch with them but use this technique to release your negative connections with them.

Command the healing energy to bless your current relationship if you have one. Command it to remove any blockages and negativities.

Feel the peace and calm settle within you. Smile.

Step 5: When you are ready, teleport yourself back to your chair from the energy plane.

Smile and open your eyes.

Feel the peace and joy within.

NOTE: Many people send positive vibes to others and don't realize that when they do so, they are energetically connecting with the other person. This connection can sometimes cause an exchange of energy and you may be impacted by their negative energy or vice versa, causing more trouble than good. Just a point of note for those who practice this. I suggest you teleport yourself to a positive energy plane as suggested in the meditation above and then bless or send positive vibes to others. This will protect you from any interchange of energies.

Within a week of carrying out the above meditation, my relationship with my colleague improved. Unless we are really good at hiding our thoughts, we subconsciously give out negative vibes through our body language and our expressions, and don't even realize it. The other person picks up on these cues and reacts to them, leading to more tension. When you send someone positive vibes, you're also breaking your own barriers and changing the way you react to the other person.

While we are on this topic, I'd also like to suggest that you use the meditation mentioned above if you're going for an interview or need to attend an important meeting that you're nervous about. Bless your meetings and interviews and the people you will see. It doesn't matter if you do not know their names or what they look like. See how your meetings go! When we bless others with positivity, our energy and attitude towards them changes. This change shows through our behavior, actions, expressions, and body language. In turn, their behavior, attitude, action, and expression toward us changes and leads to the positive experience we want.

I have been through a few relationship challenges and break-ups and want to share one of my experiences that changed my point of view.

One of my ex-partners broke down every barrier I had created around me. I was in love and completely vulnerable when I found out that we were not really together. I felt betrayed and angry. I was upset. The next few months were difficult, but I learned to detach, somewhat. I started writing for the first time and I realized what I did not want in my life. When this person came back into my life, surprisingly, my guard did not go up. Instead, I learned that I must accept people for who they are and not what I expect them to be. I realized that I had fallen in love with an image of this person and that this image was far from reality. It was a figment of my fantasy and of my expectations of my partner. I learned to let go of that image. This person was not as affable, generous, loving, or giving as I thought. Moreover, the challenges and emotional drama continued. I left the relationship.

When I have deeply loved someone and things haven't worked out, it has caused me pain and suffering, as it would to anyone else. Through this pain and suffering, I have grown and learned lessons that helped me neutralize my negative karma with a person and/or has advanced me towards my goals and aspirations. The greater the pain, the faster, and higher my growth - mentally, emotionally, and spiritually.

So…

Should I then be angry with those I have loved and lost, for helping me grow faster?

Should I be angry at them for helping me neutralize my negative karmas with them?

Or should I thank their soul for helping me grow so much so quickly?

I choose to thank them… in my meditations, irrespective of whether I remain in contact with them. Many people don't get to this point of objective assessment of their relationship breakups until they have gone through the emotions of it. Some get to the point of objectivity faster than others and if you're one of those people, be compassionate toward those who don't or can't. They are simply taking a little longer to learn to deal with the situation and cope with it. Sometimes, situations that seem simple to us can be significantly challenging to others. Similarly, the other person might find some of your difficult challenges to be easy -- another reason we must refrain from judging people's abilities and capabilities. Different people have different lessons to learn and challenges to face.

To be our own Superhero we must learn to be compassionate toward others.

The last decade has seen several changes and challenges—political, economic, and environmental, and there are possibly more to come. They will keep happening until we elevate our group consciousness and transform ourselves. This is our opportunity to help ourselves and this world we live in. I have seen and personally experienced people who take advantage of those who are seeking to transform themselves. Such situations are devastating emotionally, mentally, and spiritually. I hope this book will empower you, so you do not fall prey to such organizations and their leaders. Become your own Superhero, your own guru. And be wary of those who take advantage of others in the name of spirituality, religion or any other form of organized anything for that matter.

A Superhero must be empowered to make decisions and be wary of those who take advantage of others.

8 ACCEPT OR REGRET

The Jolly Wally's Visit to Heaven

The Jolly Wally woodcutter's soul traveled to the gates of heaven where it stood in line to be let in. When it was his turn, just like everyone else, the gatekeeper asked him one question.

"*Do you accept your death?*" *she said, calmly.*

The woodcutter thought for a moment.

"*What if I do?*"

"*Then you will be let into heaven.*"

The woodcutter thought a little more.

"*And if I don't, will I... then return to my wife and children?*"

The gatekeeper laughed.

"*You shall return to a never-ending emotion of death until you come to accept it,*" *she said.* "*Next!*"

"*No wait! I accept! I accept!*" *cried out the woodcutter.*

***

Unfortunately, saying that you accept something does not truly mean you have accepted it. True acceptance must come from a deeper place. I have struggled with acceptance. It has been one of my biggest lessons, so I feel for you if you're struggling with it too. It took me time to even realize that acceptance was one of my lessons. It began with areas of vanity, from acceptance of being a lanky teenager to acceptance of being overweight in my early 30's. Besides that, I have also struggled with acceptance of myself and my father. I remember looking for father figures in my friends' parents and in older men all through my childhood days. As I got older, I began to realize that I had developed super-high expectations of my father and he could not stack up to them. Eventually, I gave up. The expectations I had set for him were expectations I had set for myself, because I'm very much like him. Despite the lack of closeness with my father, I have always strived to make him proud of me, first through good grades in school and later, through my successes at work.

If I made a list of all my lessons in the last three decades, clearly acceptance has been in my top three and certainly a pattern for me. The challenge with acceptance is, the lack of it creeps up through our behaviors and attitude, and we don't realize it. But others who interact with us notice our little nuances in speech, tone, body language, and interactions. For example, my friends noticed that I always talked very highly and fondly of my mother but when the conversation drifted to my father, I did not have much to say. My lovers and partners noticed that I did not mention my father much when I spoke about family. I never introduced him to them. My acceptance of my father has taken me many years but there are a few practices that have helped me through the process. I'd like to share them with you.

Understanding that traits I disliked in my father were traits I disliked in myself. This was an eye opener for me. I was simply projecting my anger at not being able to change myself onto him. I was blaming him for my challenges with anger, anxiety and emotions, as we so commonly do with our parents.

Becoming aware that I wished to make peace with my father and requesting the Universe to assist me. If you ask you shall receive. I completely believe it; whether you ask God or your prophet or any higher being you believe in, the faith and openness to making a positive change is met with guidance and assistance.

Understanding the underlying reasons behind his behaviour and traits – and mine! My mother played a big role in helping me understand my father's behaviour and that made me realize that she too had gone through this acceptance phase. Much of it is attributed to his childhood, his family and the circumstances he grew up in. I do not blame any of them, but it helps me understand. With understanding comes acceptance. My experience of accepting myself has also helped me be more compassionate toward my father.

Value mapping to accept myself. This chapter focuses on providing you with a value mapping tool which is a simple yet effective way to map one's top 10 values. These values underlie the decisions we make as well as provide hints for the emotions we feel.

One of my experiences has been especially instrumental in helping me accept my father. I mentored a young man who is challenged with writing and learning disabilities. Through him, I understood how my father had struggled through in his childhood and adolescence. (My father is dyslexic). I recognized the reasons he had built up fears. The experience of mentoring also showed me that while I thought I was trying to help the young man; I was truly helping myself. This is usually true for everyone who mentors and coaches.

It is important to state the distinction between acceptance and tolerance. Acceptance is accepting reality, not accepting bad behavior and abuse from others. If you think you are accepting your partner's abusive behavior as part of compromise in your relationship, you're mistaken. You are tolerating it and letting it hurt you. Compromises are necessary in any relationship but not at the cost of your physical, emotional, or mental health. If you truly love the other person, have open communication about it and discuss it. Find solutions together. And if the other person is not willing to change then you know that you must move on.

My process of acceptance began many years ago. At first, I thought it was others' fault that I could not accept them or their behaviors. As I went through my late teenage years, I began to realize that I was rejecting friends for behaviors and traits that were similar to ones I disliked in myself. This was similar to my relationship with my father. By rejecting my friends, I was trying to reject the trait in myself.

There is yet another reason that I have disconnected with several people over the years and that has to do with conflicting values. As we get older, with experience and wisdom, our values undergo a level of transformation. We no longer believe or connect with some elements of the past and that includes some connections we had in the past. The value system is key to understanding how we think, prioritize, make decisions, and also connect with other people. It is also a system that enables us to understand who we truly are and determine metrics that make up our success criteria.

Let's say, one of your top values is honesty and you are with someone who constantly lies about little things. At first, your love or lust for this person may help you overlook this contradiction to your value but over time, you may have sudden outbursts of emotions like anger or sadness. Little things may start to bother you. Irritate you. You wonder why those things did not bother you before, or if you had overlooked them. You wonder if your work is taking a toll on your relationship. Some begin to feel anxious around their partners. Your subconscious is communicating the misalignment of values to you through emotions. Extraneous differences like habits or behaviors can be remedied through discussion but a challenge to a value will require a deeper dive, starting with the articulation of the value system.

There is a reason why many highly successful, wealthy, and famous people have feelings of dissatisfaction and restlessness. Either they have not fully aligned with their true purpose or they have not been working in alignment with their inner value system. This chapter focuses on the value map that is at the crux of acceptance. While many books and articles talk about self-love, getting to that stage requires an understanding and awareness of one's value map, one's underlying values.

I have used the value map effectively with many of my mentees to help them with their careers, relationships, and goals. It is a tool used by many cognitive therapists and coaches, and you can find several versions online. Some even have online apps. I have included a simple version of value mapping combining concepts that I have researched and experienced myself. A tool for value mapping is available at www.beyoursuperhero.org.

Finding one's true purpose is important and being aware of one's value map is critical. The two together help you become your Superhero. One without the other will not remedy your restlessness. The value map can help with several key areas of your life including:
- Gaining a deeper understanding of who you are,
- Finding the path you must take (in keeping with your true

purpose covered in 'Finding your true purpose')
- Making objective decisions in personal and professional settings
- Assessing why your current job may or may not be working for you, and understanding what needs to change.
- Assessing why your current relationship may or may not be working for you, and what needs to change.
- Determining your personal definition of success and assessing yourself
- Helping you motivate others on your team, as well as your children, siblings, friends, or others
- And more!
- So, are you ready to plot your value system?

Before we begin the value mapping exercise, I recommend a meditation.

Meditation #6: Aligning with your subconscious to enable value mapping
If you'd like to experience a guided audio version, please go to www.beyoursuperhero.org.

Step 1: Sit on a chair with your feet flat on the floor, hands on your knees, palms facing upward and spine straight, shoulders relaxed. Be comfortable on the chair. You can also do this lying on your bed as long as you keep your spine straight. Take a few deep breaths and settle into the chair.

Step 2: Visualize the energy from the Earth's core penetrating through your feet. Feel a pull on your feet as the energy enters and rises through your legs to the rest of your body. See the energy move through your meridians, organs, muscles, bone and tissue to all parts of your body and your auras – physical, mental, and emotional.
Remember energy follows thought and intention.
Command the core's energy to destroy and remove all

negative feelings, emotions, negativities, negative thoughts, anxieties, sadness, grief, anger, all lower negative emotions and feelings. Command the energy to destroy and remove any negative entities.

Take deep breaths and allow the core's energy to remove all negativities from you.

Step 3: Teleport yourself to a higher energy plane of bright light lemon yellow colored light with patches of violet color.

Bask in this higher plane and bless yourself with its bright light.

Open the energy gateway on top of your head (crown chakra) and allow the energy to enter. Allow it to mingle with the Earth's core inside you and together, they destroy and disintegrate all negativities, negative entities, negative energies inside you.

Allow your body, skin, tissue, bones, mental, emotional and physical auras to absorb the bright white light.

Step 4: Thank the universe for helping you. Ask the Universe and your subconscious mind to enable the value mapping exercise. Thank them to help you determine values that will benefit you in your current and future life. Thank them for helping you align your values with your purpose.

Step 5: Teleport yourself back to your chair from the higher energy plane.

Smile and open your eyes.

Feel the peace within yourself. Feel the gratitude.

Tool #3: Plotting your value system
Step 1: Identify your current positive values and those you would like to cultivate in the future.

Begin step 1 by circling all of your positive values/traits and the values/traits you'd like to cultivate in the future. Below is a list of values. Please feel free to add more. Pick no more than twenty values. It does not matter how high or low you'd score on them if assessed but these are values you want. In Step 3, you will have the opportunity to identify values/traits that you currently possess but do not wish to continue in your future.

Remember: These are values and traits you wish to possess in future.

Table of Values: They fall under seven categories, although some values go across categories.

Abundance	Attitude	Physical	Leadership
Wealth	Confident	Health	Leader
Success	Fun	Strength	Resilient
Fame	Respectful	Popular	Integrity
Popular	Passionate	Athletic	Compassion
Peace	Generous	...	Objective
Wisdom	Extrovert	...	Righteous
Positive	Introvert		Strategic
Freedom	Independent		Success
Joy	Liberal		Wisdom
Healer	Focused		Confident
Serious	Conservative		Tactical
Giving	Laugh		Dominating

Mental	Emotional	Others
Sharp	Loyalty	Family
Intelligent	Objective	Environment
Honest	Happy	Friendships
Wit	Love	Travel
Smart	Funny	Fun
Courage	Chillaxed	Practical
Calm	Laugh	Cool
Brave	Lonely	Negative
Risk-taker	Selfish	Risk-averse
Logical	Restless	Rational
Shy	Fiery	Cynic
Stoic	...	...

Now that you have circled all the positive values you wish

to possess, take a moment to read through this list.

Step 2: Prioritize your list to pick your top ten (Yes, only ten). For each of the values you have selected, self-score their importance to you. A score of 1 to 3 is a low, a score of 4 to 6 is a medium and a score of 7 to 10 is a high. Read through the list and update the scores if you need to. You can use numbers or 'Low,' 'Medium,' and 'High.'

#	Your top 20 Values	Importance Score (1-10)
1		
2		
3		
4		
5		
6		
7		
8		
9		
10		
11		
12		
13		
14		
15		
16		
17		
18		
19		
20		

Use the scoring to determine your top values. If the above exercise does not give you your top ten, then write your values on pieces of paper. Place them side by side. If you have post-it, stick them on a wall, one below the other in order of importance to you. Then, ask yourself the following questions:

Is #1 more important to me than #2? If not, switch their position.

Is the new #2 more important than #3? If not, switch their position.

You see where I'm going with this?

If you can't make up your mind about a couple of them, place them next to each other. Pick your top ten.

Remember, this is your value system today and what you wish for in your near future. A few years from now, you may get married, you may have children, and your value and priorities can change. I recommend doing this exercise once a year -- perhaps as a new year's resolution.

What are your top ten from the list above?

1	
2	
3	
4	
5	
6	
7	
8	
9	
10	

Step 3: Identify unwanted values/traits that you currently possess.

Pick five words from the list that represent values you currently possess but do not want in your future. Use the list of values provided above and feel free to add to it.

1	
2	
3	
4	
5	

These are important to know because they help you understand yourself better. Knowing your strengths and weaknesses will help you be more realistic when you set goals and expectations. It is important to be optimistic and be realistic -- be an optimistic realist.

Many of us struggle with accepting our weaknesses and coming to terms with areas we are challenged with, areas we need to work on. It is possible that these areas are not connected with your top ten values today, and if so, then you can ignore them for now. But be mindful that when your value system undergoes changes in future, some of these traits and behaviors or challenges may need to be looked at. And you will need to create some action items for yourself to help you deal with them.

Tool #4: Assess current job alignment:
To assess whether your current job is aligned with your values, you can use the following exercise.

Example: Let's assume that confidence is my top value and I gave it a self-evaluation score of 7. If I'm dealing with a challenging boss at work who drains my confidence, I'd place a '–' in my Current Job Score for confidence as shown below.

#	Values	Self-evaluation score (1-10)	Current job score (-/+)
1.	Confidence	7	+
2.	Fun	3	--

If fun is another value in my top 10 and I scored it at a 3 but my job gives me more opportunities to have fun, then I would give it a + job score as shown above. Fill the table below with your top ten values, your self-evaluation scores, and then your current job score to see how your job aligns with your value system. You could give your job score a number instead of a +/- but either way, it should help you get a sense of alignment of your work with your values.

#	List your Values	Self-evaluation score (1-10)	Current job score (-/+)
1.			
2.			
3.			
4.			
5.			
6.			
7.			
8.			
9.			
10.			

Tool #5: Assess current relationship alignment:
You can also use the above template to review the alignment of your relationship with your values. It may show you reasons why you're having troubles with your relationship or on the contrary, it may also show you that your relationship is solid when viewed through alignment of your values and perhaps you are being overly critical of your partner or nit-picky about things that don't really score in your top ten values.

It would be interesting to have your partner plot his or her value system too and go through a similar exercise. This will enable you to determine how aligned you two are with your values. If you find any misalignments, it would make for a good discussion on how to remedy them, through specific actions.

For example, if confidence is one of my top 10 values and my partner makes me feel more confident, then I would place a + for my relationship score. If fun was a value in my list, but I'm the one who is constantly pushing for more fun activities, I may place a − against the relationship score. Use your own judgment to fill in the table below.

#	List your Values	Self-evaluation score (1-10)	Relationship score (-/+)
1.			
2.			
3.			
4.			
5.			
6.			
7.			
8.			
9.			
10.			

If you do find any misalignments in your relationship, discuss with your partner and come up with two to three action points to help it realign with your values.

#	Your Success Values	Self-evaluation score (1-10)	Aspirational Score (-/+)
1.			
Action 1			
Action 2			
Action 3			
2.			
Action 1			
Action 2			
Action 3			
3.			

Action 1	
Action 2	
Action 3	
4.	
Action 1	
Action 2	
Action 3	
5.	
Action 1	
Action 2	
Action 3	

Tool #6: Assess options for decision-making:
Let's say I'm struggling to decide whether I should move back to the US (Option 1) or remain in New Zealand (Option 2). My top three values are as shown below.

#	Your Values	Self-evaluation score (1-10)	Option 1 Score	Option 2 Score
1	Confidence	7	7	8
2	Fun	3	7	5
3	Growth	8	8	6

From a confidence perspective, NZ scores higher than the US because, 1) I have worked in the US, which is a bigger market and my experience and expertise from the US is valued in NZ, 2) More recently I have been working in NZ, where I have built my credibility and network. So, my confidence level in NZ is high at an 8. If I returned to the US, I will need to rebuild my network and my credibility in the US and hence it is scored slightly lower at a 7.

I scored US high on Fun because New York has a lot more activities and avenues of fun than Auckland. However, New Zealand has better work life balance, so I get to enjoy time off more in Auckland than in New York. Hence, I gave the US a 7 and not a 9 or 10.

I scored US at an 8 for growth because work opportunities and prospects in my line of work is higher in the US are higher than in New Zealand. The market in the US is also much bigger than NZ.

#	Your Values	Self-evaluation score (1-10)	Option 1 Score	Option 2 Score
1				
2				
3				
4				
5				
6				
7				
8				
9				
10				

Tool #7: Motivating others:
I get asked questions about motivation all the time and ways to motivate teams/individuals who are not self-motivated. When you are in a project environment or running a program, be it business-related or creative, there will times when your team members are not motivated. Some may not appreciate activities that seem mundane, especially if they are activities that are repetitive. Others may not want to take on responsibilities. Some may want more intellectual stimulation, others may not

want to work their brains. Some want more creativity. So how do you deal with members in your team who are not motivated?

Step 1: Start with understanding.

Ask the question: What do you think your role is on this project?

Make a list of four to five bullet points.

Check to see if this list coincides with your expectations of the role. If a key expectation is missing, discuss it.

To avoid such situations, it is best to discuss expectations up front, at the start of any project so all parties have clarity on support needed and their roles and responsibilities.

Step 2: Set up a meeting to conduct a value mapping exercise.

Ask them to plot their values (up-to step 3 above). These values can go across the individual's personal and professional life. Once the value mapping is complete, you have what you need.

Step 3: Plot the role alignment with the mapped values.

For each of their top five values, brainstorm two actions in their current role/job that will align and enable the values.

For example, if one of the values is 'Strategic' but the individual is on a project that requires more tactical work, identify two things on the project that will help the individual be more strategic. It could be access to management or executives, being able to network, communicate, or conduct meetings with them, etc. These opportunities would be softer skills but important when running strategy projects with executive level stakeholders. Another action may be exposure to running meetings from time to time, setting agendas and priorities, presenting to managers and executives. Again, these are softer skills that are critical to running strategic programs for executives.

If one of the values is 'Fun' but the work really isn't, then brainstorm how the individual can add some fun to his or her work. This action may suggest activities outside of work or even leaving work early on a Friday to attend a happy hour back at the home office. It may be a breakfast setup for the team and organizing a team bonding event from time to time. Brainstorm with the person to understand what would be fun for him or her.

Step 4: Values that impact personal life

There may be certain values that are more aligned to the individual's personal life and it is best to ask if the individual is open to discussing some actions around them. The more balance between personal and professional life, the higher the motivation levels.

On completion of this exercise, you will have achieved three things:

Greater clarity on the individual's values and an understanding of his or her motivations.

Action items to help motivate the individual. Metrics that you can measure and follow up from time to time.

The individual will gain more clarity about who they are and what they're looking to achieve. They will also have more clarity on how their current job/role aligns with what they seek. This is key for motivation.

If you're unable to find ways of aligning elements of the role or job with the individual's values, then you need to look at a different role or assignment for the person. This may not sound like the best approach to many who focus on project needs over individual needs but be assured that a disgruntled and unmotivated individual will underperform on a project. Eventually, this person will leave. As leaders we are here to motivate, inspire, and help our teams.

It is also the responsibility of the team to help their leader. I find many consultants are so entangled with their own needs, they fail to see what is needed for success of their team. It is a balancing act because if one team member does not perform, it impacts everyone else.

To those who have given up their jobs and careers to take

on new ventures or creative pursuits, there will be times when you compare yourself with friends, family, ex-colleagues. Some would have moved up the corporate ladder, some bought new homes, bigger homes, some amassed a lot of wealth. While comparison is natural, it only bring us down. Instead, if you plot your value system and success metrics and then measure your progress against them, you may find that you are indeed successful. Most people seek out recognition from others for the value they create. Some do it by buying big homes, expensive cars, and talking about their fancy vacations because the appreciation of others validates their achievements. If you work toward your true purpose and make a positive impact on people's lives, irrespective of the wealth you have accumulated, the gratification from those you have helped and your inner joy will provide you with the appreciation and recognition you are seeking.

The happiness you get from buying a car or house is short-lived but the joy you get from helping others is lifelong. We must strive for joy over short-lived happiness because the former lasts longer and brings us peace and a deeper sense of achievement. It is also what this world desperately needs. Wealthy individuals must also look to strive for this deeper sense of achievement. I have met individuals who do not wish to go deeper and are happy with focusing on materialistic elements. Deep down I have found them to be insecure and dissatisfied, and that creates mental health challenges in the future. It is up to you whether you aim for this extraneous temporary feeling of satisfaction or a deep- rooted sense of accomplishment and satisfaction that will give you a sense of true value and joy.

Be your own Superhero and define your own path and success!

Tool #8: Defining success:
I find that most people define success based on wealth, awards, fame, and titles. That is how we have all been brought up. Add to that parents' expectations and competition with friends.

Many self-help books focus on wealth. While money is important to sustain a lifestyle and afford us and our families our necessities and amenities, it is not the only measure of success.

Step 1: Pick the top five or six values in your value system.

Add to this 'alignment with your true purpose' as the last component. These become your success metrics and your definition of success going forward.

To use the success metrics, begin with placing a self-evaluation score for each value – similar to the exercise we did above. A high would be a score of 8 to 10, a medium would be 5 to 7, and a low would be a 1 to 4.

Step 2: Determine an aspirational score against each value.

Refer to the table below. This score is based on where you wish to be in the near future. Be Realistic in your self-evaluation score. A realistic time-frame is 6 months or a year for achievement of the aspirational scores. This becomes your measure of success for the following year or whatever time-frame you have assigned. Your success measure and evaluation metrics are ready. But how will you get to your aspirational scores? This is where the next step comes in.

Step 3: Plot two to three action items.

Identify two to three actions for each value to take you from your self-evaluation score to your aspirational score.

After six months or a year, whatever your time frame, check your success metrics and assess if you have achieved what you had set out to achieve.

#	Your Success Values	Self-evaluation score (1-10)	Aspirational Score
1			

SUPER-ME

	Action 1:		
	Action 2:		
2			
	Action 1:		
	Action 2:		
3			
	Action 1:		
	Action 2:		
4			
	Action 1:		
	Action 2:		
5			
	Action 1:		
	Action 2:		
6			
	Action 1:		
	Action 2:		
7			
	Action 1:		

> Action 2:

Let's say, my self-evaluation score for confidence as a value, was 7 and my aspirational score was a 9. Note that some of you may score yourself higher but as long as you are making a realistic estimate, your self-evaluation will work. On assessing my confidence value, I find that I am an 8 today. It shows that I have made progress but haven't yet achieved a 9. For many, wealth may have been one of their top five values and you may have not achieved the level of wealth to which you aspire. However, you may have made progress or achieved your aspirational score on the other four or five values that make up your success criteria. You may have significantly over-achieved your alignment with your true purpose. You may not have achieved the level of wealth you wanted but you may have scored high on having fun. You may have achieved the growth you wanted in your career but not achieved the confidence you expected.

Your success must be measured against your own value system and not what you think others will measure you against. The latter is what has created a deep-rooted imbalance in expectations and added to anxieties, depression, and mental health issues.

While wealth is important, it is time that we assess our impact on society, on culture, humanity, and the environment to understand the value we generate. When we assess someone's success, we must be more interested in understanding how he or she uses wealth and fame to create true value for society and the environment.

OPTIONAL Step for Self-acceptance: To better understand yourself, you can use the series of questions below. Some questions may warrant answers similar to others in the list and many are similar to those we get asked in job interviews. So if you are preparing for a job interview, feel free to use these questions as preparation material.

What are your top three to five strengths?
What are your top three to five weaknesses?
What are your top two accomplishments in life?
What are your top two failures in life?
What are you good at?
What do you want your legacy to be?

What are some mistakes you have made in the last five years that you wish you hadn't? What have you learned from them?

What are some aspects of your personality, habits or behaviour's that you would like to change in the future?

If you could change two things about yourself, what would they be in each of the categories below?

- Physical
- Mental
- Emotional

What actions or activities give you the most joy? Why?

If your parents described you in three words, what would they be?

How would your partner describe you in three words? Your friends?

What is that one thing you are most proud of? Why?

What is the one or two things you are most embarrassed of? (Make a list and pick the top two)

Is there anything or anyone you struggle with? Why?

What are some traits in your siblings or parents that you do not appreciate? Do you have those same traits or behaviours?

What are your top three goals in life?

9 RESILIENCE

The Jolly Wally's Journey to Resilience

A young Jolly Wally spent hours meditating but could not understand the true meaning of resilience. Each time he tried, he would fall asleep. Disappointed and irritated that he had wasted so much time, he went to see his teacher.

"I have come to seek the meaning and understanding of resilience from you," he said.

The teacher smiled. "I cannot teach you that, let go of your quest," he said.

The young Wally frowned. "Then I must seek the person who can," he said.

"Wonderful," said the teacher and returned to his meditation.

Disappointed, the young Wally bid farewell to his beautiful home and the pristine green island and set out by sea. Months turned to years and one morning, the teacher was greeted by a familiar voice.

"You have returned!" said the teacher excitedly.

The young Wally had grown a beard, and his hair was thick and curled. He had lost weight and looked athletic.

"Well? Did you find your teacher?"

The young Wally shook his head.

"And the meaning of resilience?"

"No but shouldn't you let go of your eagerness to know?" said the young Wally.

The teacher burst out laughing. "Tell me about your travels," he said.

The young Wally spoke about his boat being caught in a storm and how he managed to get through it by tying himself to a float and stealing a bottle of whiskey from the captain. When the captain found out, he wanted to throw him overboard, but he made a deal with the captain to help mend his torn clothes and jacket, a skill he had learned from his father. When food rations were low, he was asked to catch his own fish and the best he could do was grab jellyfish and make soup. But the soup tasted so good with his secret ingredient that other sailors traded him fish for a bowl. Finally, after a month at sea, he reached the big island where he went looking for his teacher. Drunk sailors claiming to be teachers spoke of their adventures at sea and the young Wally wrote their stories in his diary but moved on. He would go from town to town narrating, over-dramatizing humorous stories at bars and in return receive food, alcohol, and sometimes, shelter. One evening, he was at the beach, staring into the horizon, when a passerby stopped by for a conversation with him.

"What are you looking for?" said the stranger.

"Just enjoying the view," said the young Wally.

"You look lost," said the stranger.

The young Wally smiled. It was then that he decided to return home.

"You have found resilience after all," said his old teacher. "I could have never taught you to let go and live in the present moment. Even if I did, I would not be able to instill creative thinking like you have displayed in difficult times. Most important of all, I could never teach you to have a sense of humor. But I'm curious, what was your secret ingredient in your soup?"

"Let it go master," said the young wally in a usual tone used by his teacher.

***

I returned to the US after living in New Zealand for many years and it felt like homecoming, thanks to the warm welcome of friends and family here. One of my first trips was to Florida to see my friends parents, Mrs and Mr R. They had lost their home to the Houston floods and had recently moved to Florida to live close to their daughter, her husband and two children. Now Mr. R had been suffering from back pain and spine trouble for a long time and in 2017, and after many painful episodes, he had opted for surgery. He had also had one of his knees replaced back in 2015. The day before the flood, he slipped and fell, cracking his other kneecap in two. The rains had started, it was a Friday evening, and the doctors had left town. Within hours, water began clogging the drains and bayous. Mr. R popped a few pain killers and decided to wait through the night. By then, the first floor of their home was flooded and they had to move upstairs. Much was lost and when the water receded, the house wasn't livable. Floors rotted, carpets smelled, and appliances and furniture were damaged. Most homes in the neighborhood needed to be gutted, and Mrs & Mr R ended up selling their home a few months later. In the midst of all this, Mr. R had his other knee replaced.

Now Mrs & Mr R, both in their early seventies are busy setting up their new home in Florida, working on the yard and interiors, making it their residence. They are just the same as I remember from years ago, happy, jovial, cracking jokes about themselves and enjoying life and its little pleasures. The only difference I have noticed is that they need nanna naps every afternoon.

During my journey through the Himalayas, I bumped into a seventy-five-year old man who trekked with me for fourteen kilometers up the mountain to a shrine called Kedarnath. He spoke very little while we trekked, and I presumed he was conserving energy but he did suggest taking breaks every thirty to forty-five minutes. On our first break, he mentioned he was doing the trek for the fiftieth time.

"Every year?" I gasped.

The man nodded.

"Are you a Shiva devotee?"

He shook his head.

"So... you just like the exercise?"

He smirked and then told me how he had lost his wife at an early age. I saw the love for her in his eyes as he spoke passionately about her and her spirituality. He said that it was her dream to come to Kedarnath and so every year he makes a trip in memory of her.

I felt sorry for him that he had not moved on from his wife's untimely death. As we continued our journey, I realized that I was so wrong. He had no hint of sadness about him and joked about his legs giving way, and his back. He laughed about the pain in his shoulders and then at people younger than he, being carried in palanquins.

"Do you know why I really come to this place every year?"

"For your wife?"

"Yes, of course, but also because it teaches me to be resilient. Old age requires you to be resilient. I'm glad you are practicing," he said, and laughed out loud. "This exercise is good but the best thing is laughter."

I must mention my father here too. He was about sixty, when he was diagnosed with cancer and lost some of his ability to speak. The cancer had spread to two of his lymph nodes. Doctors gave him five years. It has been twenty and he still goes for his morning walks and loves his spicy and greasy food, much to my mother's annoyance. It is no wonder that he has compassion for those who have faced adversity, gives advice that is practical, optimistic and realistic, and is able to celebrate others' successes as his own. He is a resilient man with a zest for living and life.

There is no single formula for resilience. Different people have different capacities for it, but I have observed five key traits in resilient people that are worthy of discussion.

- Strong support networks
- Gratitude
- Realistic optimism
- Humor
- The ability to let go

Many of us have these traits in some measure, and the more we hone them, the better for us. There have been times in my life where I have spent years trying to get something going, taken big risks, moved countries, only to experience failure. There is no frustration as big when you have remained optimistic, done what you needed to do, and yet fallen short of the outcome you need or want. You may deal with those failures and move on, hoping that you are moving toward the one goal you have set for yourself. But there are days when you stop and wonder if you went wrong. You compare yourself with friends who seem to have it better. You wonder if you have screwed up your career and your life just to chase after this one goal you had set for yourself.

Many creative souls can relate to this dilemma. It is not easy in the creative industry and the only thing one can do is immerse oneself into one's art. Find solace in doing what gives you joy, irrespective of commercial acceptance or recognition.

At some point, you stop thinking about the outcome and just do. This is the state of letting go. This is the state we must train ourselves to be in. Detach from outcomes and just focus on doing. I cannot promise that you will never feel doubt or frustration. But if you let those thoughts pass and return to the doing, distract yourself from thoughts about outcomes, you have taken another step towards being resilient.

The Jolly Wally Woodcutter in Heaven
Our Jolly Wally woodcutter who died and went to heaven had finished his work for the day and was resting over soft white grass when the gatekeeper showed up and handed him more work.

"But I just finished mowing this lawn today."

"Who's going to work for the baggage you have brought along?" she said and pointed to the genie sitting on a branch, munching a golden apple.

"She is the reason I'm here!" said the Jolly Wally woodcutter (Remember the ironical parable about the woodcutter's wish).

"She's not my baggage she is…"

"I don't care who does it," the gatekeeper interrupted. "You know the rules of heaven. You're responsible for your baggage's work. She certainly isn't doing it."

"Don't you have your own genie heaven to go to?" said the Jolly Wally woodcutter to the genie. "No wait, you'd go to hell!"

The genie giggled. "I would, if you would let me!"

"Let you? I want you to go!"

"You've held on to your anger toward me. It is not my fault your wish was flawed. I'm not working, so until you let me go, you're doing work for the both of us."

"Why don't you just play one of your tricks and disappear? Or get this work done."

"My tricks don't work here in heaven."

The Jolly Wally mumbled and grumbled and continued working. That night he lay in bed and thought about letting go of the genie. But the more he thought about her, the more peeved he got. He realized he was also angry at himself for not thinking through the wish he had made. He was angry for making a wish… and then he was angry at his deceased parents who had not taught him right. He blamed them for their habits, which he had emulated and for not teaching him to let go. It was their fault he had to suffer this state of death. He promised to tell them when he got to meet them in heaven.

The next morning, he woke up feeling grumpy and reached the meadow, ready to give the genie a piece of his mind. But when he got there, she was gone.

"Have you seen the genie?" he asked the gatekeeper.

"She left," said the gatekeeper.

Excited that he had let go of her, our Jolly Wally woodcutter spent all day working on a bed of lilies. When it was time to retire, the gatekeeper paid him a visit again.

"Here's your next assignment for today," said the gatekeeper.

"Two more? But I thought the genie was gone!"

"She is gone," said the gatekeeper and gestured behind him.

Standing behind him were his old parents. They had become his baggage.

***

Trait #1: The ability to let go

Letting go helps with acceptance. Many times, we convince ourselves that we have let go of an incident or event that caused pain only to be reminded again that we haven't. Little events can trigger memories or trapped emotions. Trapped because we think we have released them, but we've held on to remnants. These remnants show up in different forms through our behaviors and responses to situations and people. The only way I can let go is to completely rely on the Universe, consciously stopping myself from thinking what-if situations and worrying about the future.

This is not easy when your career depends on a decision you have to make. When you are confused about the direction you must go. You have tried weighing pros and cons for each option, but you're unsure. Your mind keeps wavering, your intuition keeps sending you doubts. Your stomach feels queasy and your anxiety takes over. Something deep down is causing you to question what you are doing. Is it fear? Is it a past experience that caused you panic? Is it anxiety associated with change? How can one let go in such situations and rely on the Universe?

Letting go does not mean giving up. It is a process of trusting yourself, the universe, higher beings, higher energy, God, prophets, or any other source you believe in. There is no single instruction for letting go but I have discussed three key elements here that have helped me with it.

I recollect another time in my life when I was challenged with letting go. I had been miserable in my job and tried to quit twice and both times, unexpected turns kept me at the job. In the first instance, I had cleared background and reference checks for a new job, but the organization delayed making me a formal offer while I was in negotiation with my current firm. I accepted a renewed offer for my current job. A few months later, I received a verbal and email offer from another firm. It was later rescinded by HR and I knew they were playing silly games. I had to take it as a sign from the Universe that I was meant to remain in my current role. I dealt with my emotions and tried to determine the lessons I was meant to learn. There were two:

- Relying on the universe
- Learning to accept and make the best of a situation. Remaining objective.

I started loving my job. How great is that?

Shit happens. It happens to all of us at some point in our lives. How we deal with it determines whether it will have a positive or negative impact on our lives. I remember a time when my efforts to look for employment just weren't working. I was qualified and, in some cases, over-qualified, diligent, hard-working and passionate about what I did, yet for whatever reason, I wasn't getting any interviews. Visa barriers began to surface and that made me wonder if I had made the right decision to move countries. Then came big expenses. Four months into the job search, you can imagine my frustration. I was in a state of limbo. I wondered if I wasn't doing enough, if

I wasn't doing the right things. If I had made the right decision, if I was overthinking it, if I wasn't thinking the right way. For weeks, I struggled with what-if situations. It only caused more anxiety and confusion. I could not meditate properly. My value map pointed to the decision I had made. Yet, I continued to feel anxious and uneasy. Something was not right and I could not figure out what. But I continued to push. I stayed on the path I had taken. Finally, it dawned upon me that I was trying to control the outcomes of my actions. I was fearful of the outcomes. There were events in the past that caused me anxiety and fear from within. What followed was a whole new level of letting go for me and I realize now that if I hadn't had this experience, I could not have created the meditation mentioned below. Neither would I understand what it feels like to be stuck, where nothing seems to be working. It made me realize that sometimes, the Universe asks us to pause and expand our consciousness. It is after we expand that we can take on more energy. If your bucket can only hold five liters and you receive twenty, you can only retain five. I needed to increase the size of my bucket; one of understanding, letting go, acceptance, and resilience. Your bucket may need expansion in other areas and only you can be the judge of it. Rely on your subconscious and your emotions to understand when there is a need to pause, assess, and accept.

There are three things that helped me let go. First, I needed to truly believe that I had access to abundance. This access to abundance was the support I was looking for. If you believe you are poor, no matter how much money you make or possess, you will feel poor and act it. If you believe you do not find success but only challenges, then you will attract the energy of challenges. If you're generally thinking negative thoughts, you will attract more negativity. This will manifest itself in the form of ailments and mental and emotional challenges. You will attract people who are negative. However, it isn't easy to feel supported when you are struggling with the exact opposite emotion. As I went through my emotions, I decided to conduct a series of experiments. By now you can probably tell that I'm analytical and I enjoy breaking down problems and determining what works and what doesn't. This, I attribute to my undergraduate degree in engineering.

So, I began my experiment by writing down three random things, I wanted to see in the next forty-eight hours: 1) a psychic, 2) a blue bird, and 3) a snake. These were the first three things that came to mind. I don't have an explanation for why those things in particular. As I meditated that morning, I suggested them to my sub-conscious mind. The following day, I received a message through social media from someone in a foreign country. This person was someone I had followed online only a few days ago. I cannot remember who added whom first, but we had common interests. In her message, she said to me that she had a reading for me and would like to share it. I had no idea she was psychic. I'm also not someone who likes to know the future and believe that those who prefer to know the future will find it harder to let go. The need to know shows the need to control future outcomes. This need to control outcomes shows a lack of reliance on the Universe. It was barely twenty-four hours since I began my experiment, and I had found a person with psychic capabilities. The very same day, I also spotted an indigo bunting in Central park, where I went walking. I hoped I would not come across a snake and stuck to wide roads. Snakes are not my favorite reptiles. That night, I opened my social media page to find a picture of a friend visiting SE Asia, holding a yellow python wrapped around her.

I undertook similar experiments a few times and each time they worked. It was clear to me that when I connect with my subconscious through meditation and request something specific, it is more tuned to seeking out and spotting these requests. This is exactly how the laws of attraction and intentions work. What we think and align with is what we will attract. You might ask if that means we attract challenges and conflict? We have already discussed in the chapter, 'No Escape' the reasons we go through challenges and conflicts. The laws of attraction work to bring us what we aspire to;

however, we may go through certain challenges if they are meant to teach and ready us for what we are about to receive. Would you give responsibility for your child to someone who is not equipped to manage children? Would you want to give responsibility for coaching you to someone who has never done it before? Then how do we expect the Universe to give us responsibility when we aren't ready for it?

To follow the laws of attraction and intuition is not easy when we're going through difficult times. This is where a meditation comes in; a meditation to align with the energy of abundance.

This meditation gave me the strength and the power to let go of my worries, rely on the universe and know that I have access to abundance in all aspects of my life. It does not matter what others think of you and your achievements, it matters what you think of them. It matters if you are at peace with yourself and feel fulfilled. That is exactly how I felt when doing this meditation from time to time.

Meditation #7: Align with abundance and let go.
This is a meditation you can do at any time of the day, but I recommend doing it while the sun is up. It is a visualization technique that does not require you to focus on your breath but instead on energizing yourself.

Key: Energy follows thought and intention. If any thoughts arise during this meditation, do not fight them but calmly disconnect from them. Say in your mind, *'Disconnect from that thought'* and then return to the meditation.

Step 1: Lie on grass (over a yoga mat) in your garden or at a quiet spot in the park. If you don't have access to either, sit on a chair in a quiet room with your feet flat on the floor, hands on your knees, and palms facing upward. Whether you are lying on the grass or sitting up on a chair, keep your spine straight, shoulders relaxed. Be comfortable. Take a few deep breaths and settle into your position.

Step 2: Visualize the energy from the Earth's core penetrating through your feet. Feel a pull on your feet as the energy enters and rises through your legs to the rest of your body. See the energy move through your meridians, organs, muscles, bone and tissue to all parts of your body and your aura – physical, mental, and emotional. (Remember energy follows intention).

If you are laying on grass, become one with the ground and the trees around you. Feel their positive energy and feel your alignment with plants, insects, birds, minerals, microorganisms, fish, and humans – all kingdoms on the planet.

Command the Earth's energy to suck out and destroy any negative feelings, emotions, negativities, negative thoughts, anxieties, sadness, grief, anger, any lower negative emotions and feelings. Negative entities. Take deep breaths and allow the Earth's energy to remove all negativities from you. Allow it to circulate through your physical, mental, and emotional bodies.

Step 3: Teleport yourself to a higher plane that is a mix light lemon-yellow and patches of light violet

If you are a visual person, you can see geometric and floral patterns in this energy plane. These patterns keep moving and changing.

Feel peaceful inside. Bask in the plane of abundance and feel joy within. Bless yourself with this energy.

You are one with the energy.

This abundance is always with you.

It has always been with you. It is with you always!

Feel the joy as you have this realization and let go of your worries and thoughts.

Bask in this energy plane as long as you need.

Step 4: Return to your chair from the higher energy plane when you are ready.

Smile and open your eyes.

You may feel drowsy and thirsty after this meditation. Take a nap and hydrate.

In addition to the above meditations, I also used tools from the chapter, 'Don't patent your patterns'. Specifically, around disconnecting from negative thoughts and emotions. Each time, I had a what-if thought, I consciously paused, recognized that I had the thought, and then disconnected from it. Then I distracted my mind with positive and productive actions like house cleaning, walking at the park, bike rides, cooking, and swimming. Instead of eating or retail therapy, focus on activities that will bring you better health and help you practice mindfulness. I also used writing as therapy. I focused on actions and activities that bring me joy – writing. I focused on my work and my true purpose. The meditation helped strengthen my faith in the Universe and build my confidence in myself. If prayer brings you this strength and peace, then pray. Some get strength from doing martial arts and I highly recommend it to those who struggle with discipline and will power. Martial arts are a great way to learn both.

There is yet another technique that has proven to be very powerful for me and my coaches and that is connecting the subconscious mind.

Technique #13: Connect with your subconscious…
A simple yet effective technique that is available to all.

Sit on a chair in a meditative position like that mentioned in the book. Take a few deep breaths and calm yourself. Settle into the chair.

With intention tell yourself to connect with your subconscious mind. Disconnect from your conscious mind and connect with your subconscious.

Breathe into this thought and feel a sense of calm and peace settle inside you.

Next, touch your heart and ask your subconscious mind to activate your heart chakra (energy gateway) and then command you heart chakra to manage the solar plexus (just above the naval where you feel your anxiety) and ajna (point between your eyes).

Command your heart chakra to kick in each time you begin to feel anxious or confused. Command your subconscious mind to help you gain your peace and calm.

Ultimately, while a Superhero must be aware of several tools and techniques he or she must put them to good use to truly feel empowered and access the strength and energy within. Gain support from the Universe.

Trait #2: A strong support network

Another important trait I have noticed in resilient people is their support networks. You don't need a hoard of supporters, but research has shown that reaching out to friends and family helps with resilience. It helps us deal with challenges better. It makes sense. When I'm challenged, I connect with my parents and my close friends, discuss my challenges with them, get their feedback and input before I make a decision. There is no better service than to help someone in need – without an ulterior motive, of course. I have noticed I may be a helping hand to someone in need, but they may not reciprocate. At times, they are unwilling, and at times they are not capable of helping me. I do, however, receive help from others in my network. The Universe always sends someone or a tool or technique my way to help me through the challenge. To avail myself of this tool or technique, I must be open to receiving it. And be grateful to the Universe for sending me the help when I need it.

Research has shown that the more we isolate ourselves, the more helpless we feel and the higher the incidence of substance abuse. If you do not have family or friends nearby, reach out to your community or non-profits through helplines available online.

If you seek help from family or friends, remember that everyone is busy and unless you are clear about how you feel and where you need assistance, they may not understand. Refrain from assuming that your family or friends will understand what you're going through without you telling them so. Refrain from expecting them to be open to your challenging behaviors and conversations. Do not take them for granted. You are seeking their help, so seek it in a way that is amicable and acceptable to all, not in an intrusive and demanding manner. I have seen many people lean on their parents, as if it is the parents' fault that they're facing a challenge.

Trait #3: Gratitude
You might ask, why be grateful when the universe could do better and not put me in that difficult situation at all. The challenge or conflict is helping expand my consciousness or teaching me a skill or lesson I need. It is up to me to accept it or make life more difficult for myself. I accept the challenges. We have covered gratitude in 'Make a wish'.

Trait #4: Realistic optimism
Being optimistic is great but when you face a challenge, you need to be realistic. It is seen that optimistic people go through challenges with hope when their optimistic and unrealistic expectation is met with failure. They feel helpless. When hope is challenged, and helplessness sets in, our immune system and body is challenged, leading to diseases and health issues. A realist will look to make the best of a situation and use creative ways of dealing with it. A realist has faith and hopes for the best but also knows that actions must be taken to stay afloat. They may have faith in God or a higher being, the Universe or themselves. But realists are mindful of the environment they're in. They'll take on a temporary job to pay their bills while making a career change or looking for something more permanent.

Realists are also more creative in their actions. For example, if you have tried to look for a job and haven't succeeded, then you need to change strategy. Clearly continuing to do what you're doing will not give you a different outcome. Most times, people send out the same resume for different jobs with a customized cover letter. While the customization of the cover letter helps, it is also important to write your resume differently for, say, a non-profit organization vs. a for-profit one, the role of a management consultant vs. the role in a corporate setup even though the job might require the same skills and experiences. If posting your resume for job applications online is not working, then you need to change tactics. Use online channels to reach out to people in firms where you want to work and ask them for a phone conversation or a coffee appointment. Most people are willing to give advice when they have the time. Ask for advice and then request a referral. Be prepared to ask the right questions and be ready for an informal interview. If you are feeling stuck and out of ideas, reach out to your support network and ask them. Brainstorm.

Trait #5: Humor

People who have a good sense of humor are also the most resilient. Their humor may be cheesy, absurd, dry, slapstick; it doesn't matter. It is humor that keeps them going. The ability to laugh at one's situation is perhaps the best way to deal with a challenge and help yourself be more resilient. Many are able to joke and laugh about their situations after the fact. It is not after but during that helps us the most. There is science behind it. Laughter releases endorphins, the feel-good hormone. It also re-activates our pre-frontal lobe that is responsible for objective decision making. When the pre-frontal lobe takes over, it can break the pattern of an emotional downer.

A few years ago, my father came home all excited and announced that he was going to join the 'Ha-ha' club for retired citizens. According to him, the group gathers in a circle in a park or garden and then forces laughter, as loudly as they possible can. Seeing people laugh makes others laugh and this chain reaction continues. After five minutes, the team disperses and goes along their daily morning routines. I think it is a fantastic idea.

When you are feeling low and are alone in a quiet place, try laughing out loud. No one is around to watch you or laugh at you. As you laugh loudly, you will begin to find it ridiculous and funny and laugh at yourself laughing, and the cycle will continue for a bit. Some may feel a sudden need to cry and that is fine too. It will help release your emotion. But try to laugh as hard and as long as you possibly can. Do stop if your jaw starts hurting. If you can't force laughter, then watch standup comedy or a series that you know is super funny. You need a hearty laughter, not muffled smirks.

A Superhero understands the power of fun and laughter and makes it a point to make time for them. A Superhero understands the need for balance in one's professional and personal life. We ourselves are responsible for our own lives and how we lead them. Empower yourself so you can lead a fulfilled life.

Here is a visualization technique to helping you become more resilient.

Technique #14: Visualization and cognition combination
This is similar to the visualization technique discussed in Chapter 3 and uses a combination of visualization and cognition to help you deal with your challenge.

Pre-Work: Your current situation may be causing you anxiety, fear, or depression. It may be bringing up insecurities from the past. You need an effective way to release your emotions and remain objective, so you can tackle your situation. Keep your patience and persevere.

Before we begin, it is important to assess your past experiences and identify any events from the past that may have caused you the emotions you are currently feeling. They may be similar events or different but the emotion was the same. If you are unable to determine other events, that's okay too. Let's assume you have identified one other event from the past that caused you to lose confidence and your resilience.

Step 1: Get into a meditative state.

Sit on a chair with your feet flat on the floor and spine straight, shoulders relaxed. Hands on your knees with palms facing upward.

Visualize the energy of the Earth's core entering your feet and traveling through your legs to your hips and upper body. You may feel a pull on your feet.

For more visual people, you may visualize a color – say light green. Flush your body with the core's energy and command it to suck out any negativity, negative entities, negative energies from your physical, mental, and emotional auras. This is also your connection to the planet and will keep you grounded through the meditation.

Step 2: Next, teleport yourself to the plane of abundance high above the Earth.

For those who are more visual, see this plane with light lemon-yellow energy laced with patches of light violet. Float inside this energy plane and bask in it. Absorb the energy through your crown chakra (on top of your head) and through your skin, into your muscles, bones and tissue. You may feel a tingling sensation.

Allow yourself to absorb the abundance of joy, peace, health, wealth, success, and love.

Step 3: Remain inside the healing plane. Visualize feeling calm, joyful, and centered.

Bring up the event from the past and visualize it in front of you, as if you're watching it on a live screen. Watch people associated with the event tell you things that caused you anxiety or the negative emotion. If it wasn't a conversation, visualize the event happening in front of you or see the people who caused it standing, facing you.

See yourself undeterred by their conversation, revelations, or presence. You smile and remain calm as you watch. You feel strong and confident that you are able to remain calm and peaceful. You feel compassion and unconditional love for the people just as you feel for everyone else in need. You can remain there as long as you want, feeling strong, calm, peaceful, and joyous, undeterred by the event or the people. When you are ready, you leave the event and people and walk into a doorway that is filled with bright sparkling light lemon-yellow light. It is the doorway to abundance. You enter and bask in this abundance energy. Smile and feel the joy of feeling strong, peaceful, and calm.

Repeat this step for your current situation.

Then teleport yourself back to your chair. And feel the calm, peace, joy, and love settle inside you.

It can sometimes take one to two days to notice the impact of this exercise, depending on the depth of the challenge you are currently facing. An emotional release may also occur during these two days. Allow the emotions to pass. It is part of your healing. See how you go.

10 FINDING YOUR TRUE PURPOSE

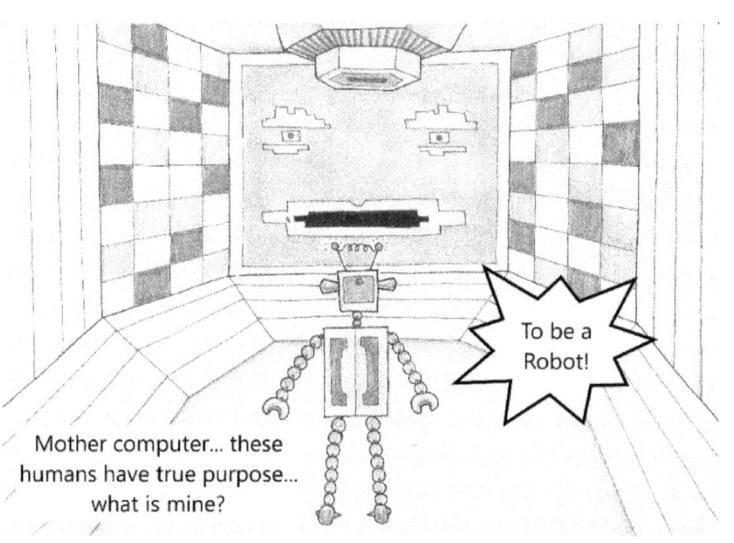

The Jolly Wally's Pursuit for True Purpose

A young and creative Jolly Wally set out to find his true purpose in life. He loved to paint and make sculptures and designs, but he couldn't figure out his true purpose. He went from one city to another in search of his purpose until he reached the home of an old Jolly Wally jeweler.

"Want to give me a hand with these designs?" said the old Wally. "I'll let you stay the night and have a good meal if you do."

"Sure," said our young Wally, who was always up for helping others. Together they made beautiful jewelry and the old Wally appreciated how quickly the Jolly Wally had picked up the skill.

"Why don't you stay with us and become my apprentice?" said the old Wally.

The young Wally accepted the offer but months went by and he suddenly decided he was going to leave.

"I must find my true purpose," he said and set out again.

It was stormy weather and he had to take shelter at a stranger's home that night. The stranger had a beautiful daughter and seeing her the Jolly Wally's heart melted. He decided to return one day to ask for her hand in marriage, after he had found his purpose. The next morning, as he set out again, he met a beggar.

"I'm sorry but I only have this food that the beautiful Wally packed for me. You may have it," he said to the beggar.

Days went by and the Jolly Wally continued on his journey but was starting to get frustrated when he bumped into a genie in the woods.

"Why are you in such distress?" she said with a giggle.

"I am looking for my true purpose."

"Deep," she said and giggled again.

"Have you found yours?" said the Wally, irritated by her mockery.

She nodded. "To make wishes come true for those who ask."

The Jolly Wally's eyes lit up. "Would you grant me a wish then? Help me find my true purpose?"

"Granted," said the genie and flew away.

The Jolly Wally stood there wondering if anything had changed. He asked himself if he found his true purpose, but the response was the same. Disappointed and frustrated, he turned around to go home. On the way he stopped by the jeweler to pay his respects.

"Have you found your true purpose?" asked the jeweler.

The young Wally shook his head.

"I'm getting old and don't have a son. If you help me, I shall let you have a share of the profits," said the old one.

The Jolly Wally agreed and became his business partner. As months went by, he thought of the young woman and decided to pay her a visit. He gifted her one of his designs on a piece of wood. It didn't matter that he had not gifted her gold. She was so taken by his creativity that she fell in love and the two decided to get married. The day of the wedding, the Jolly Wally set out to the girl's town and on the way, he met the same beggar he had seen before.

"Have you found your true purpose?" said the beggar.
The Jolly Wally shook his head but gave him pieces of gold coins so he could build himself and his family a shelter and feed his children. The beggar blessed him and his soon to be wife and the Jolly Wally continued. But when he got to the girl's home, he was in for a surprise.

"I cannot let you marry my daughter unless you have found your true purpose," said the father of the bride. "What if you leave again?"

The Jolly Wally was in a fix. He thought hard but could not figure out his true purpose. Just then the genie appeared.

"Why are you always sad when I see you? Do you not have anything better to do?" she said.

"It is all your fault. You didn't grant me my wish."

The genie laughed. "That is not possible," she said. "Now tell me everything that has happened since I last saw you."

The Jolly Wally narrated his journey in the last few months. The genie listened intently and then giggled again.

"My job is only to grant wishes, not to coach silly and sad, Jolly Wallys. But because you doubt my power, I ask you a question. Did you not use your passion for creativity to make beautiful jewelry that won you love and enabled you to help those in need?"

The Jolly Wally's eyes lit up and he realized that the genie has spelled out his true purpose.

***

During my journey through the Himalayas, I met several yogis. In fact I went around in search of my guru to help me determine my purpose in life. I had this notion that I was meant to go on this journey to find my teacher. And that my teacher would tell me what I was meant to do and become.

"You are wasting your time," shouted a yogi from behind.

"Excuse me?" I said and then ignored him.

The yogi laughed.

"What are you looking for?" he said.

Not you! I thought.

"Just traveling," I lied to avoid conversation.

"You won't find what you are looking for. The more you look the farther you will go from it. Find your purpose instead. I can tell that your purpose is not being on the mountains."

At this point I was annoyed by his advice but nodded and left. Like I mentioned earlier, I never found my guru on the mountains. I also did not find my true purpose. A few months later, I decided to volunteer with a non-profit organization as a teacher for underprivileged children. On my first day, I taught a group of eight to ten-year-olds, and it was fascinating to see them eager to learn and ask lots of questions. They were hungry for information and knowledge. They wanted more! They emulated my accent, attentively listened to math tricks, and laughed at my silly stories from around the world. After I finished the session and got into my car, I felt a sudden surge of emotions that brought tears to my eyes, and my heart was filled with joy. It was a feeling of gratefulness for the opportunity. I knew then that I must empower and help youth and adults. I found my purpose when I stopped obsessing about it. However, subconsciously I was still looking for it.

My true purpose is to empower people with leadership and life lesson skills, and I do so through various means. This book is part of my true purpose and brings me joy.

I'd like to point out the difference between happiness and joy here. Happiness can be short-lived. You purchase a fancy car and you are happy for some time. You purchase jewelry and it makes you temporarily happy. When you do something for someone, you feel joy within your heart: A strong and abiding feeling of security, peace, love, and contentment. Think of the last time you did something nice for someone without wanting anything in return from him or her. Try to remember that feeling. That is the feeling we must all aspire to. Whatever made you feel that way is probably connected to your passion and your true purpose.

I met a young man in his twenties who suffers from challenges in mobility and speech, but he does not let it affect him. When I asked him how he found his true purpose he said it was all the teasing and bullying in school that helped. He decided he would not return to his high school and instead focused his time and effort on being happy with who he was. He now shares his experiences through workshops and presentations with others. He certainly is someone who brings light and inspires courage in others. That to me is his true purpose.

Sometimes we find our true purpose through adversities. Someone I know spent over ten years training and working with an esoteric organization and during her last couple of years with them, she felt suppressed and stifled. The management team took advantage of people and manipulated them using fear. She said she felt like she was not growing –in fact, her self-esteem and confidence were shrinking. Despite many difficulties, she left. She learned that she needed to reclaim her inner strength, her inner power. She dealt with fears that had been instilled in her over time. It took a few months, but she bounced back and started to explore aspects of inner healing through naturopathy and nutrition. She has now started an innovative and holistic approach to healing people through foods, naturopathy, and other alternative approaches. This is an example of finding one's true purpose through challenging situations.

When I asked my mother what her true purpose is, she instantly said it was to raise her children to be good Samaritans. If anyone knows her personally, they would agree that she is someone who can heal people through her words, thoughts, and prayers. But she does not see healing as her true purpose. Supporting and helping others who work toward positive causes can also be one's true purpose.

If you run a business that creates a livelihood for a number of people, then you are impacting not only those lives but also the lives connected to them. As a leader, you have responsibility toward those who support you and follow you. You might want to run a successful business or be a leader in a certain industry and by doing so, you have the opportunity to positively impact lives of many people. Or you may create products that positively impact the environment. Running a successful business to positively impact lives and the environment can be your true purpose.

If you are of the notion that simply making money is your purpose, then I would suggest you speak to successful people who have accumulated wealth. They will tell you that making money is not one's true purpose. Financial gain can never be one's true purpose unless it's coupled with using the money to serve the five kingdoms on this planet, namely, humans, plants, animals (insects, animals, bird, and fish), minerals and microorganisms.

A friend of mine from the US was traveling through China with her father when she had a dream. In this dream, she saw herself working with children and youth, developing programs to help them with overall development. When she woke up the next morning, she had made up her mind. She applied to and go through an Ivy League University to pursue a Doctorate and currently works with programs for children and youth. She found her true purpose through a dream.

Tool #9: Finding your true purpose:
Step 1: Begin this exercise with a meditation below to align with your subconscious mind so you can determine and align with your true purpose.

Meditation #8: Aligning with one's true purpose
Here is a visualization/meditation technique you can use to find and align with your true purpose in life. This meditation is also available at www.beyoursuperhero.org.

Remember: Energy follows thought.
Duration: 10 minutes
When to use this technique:
- To align with your true purpose and seek guidance for a challenge you are facing
- Need guidance on any life path related decisions,
- To understand your life's purpose
- Allow your soul to take you through the path you truly deserve

Preferred Time: Early morning after a bath or shower
Preferred location: Anywhere quiet

Getting into the zone...
Sit on a chair with your feet flat on the floor and spine straight. Your palms on your knees facing upward. Close your eyes and take a few deep breaths. Release any tension you have in your body. Any pain, physical, emotional or mental, any stress, grief, anxiety, fears, and all negativities and negative energies.

If your mind is distracted at any point during this meditation, calmly bring it back to focus on your breath. Feel your body relax into your posture. Relax your shoulders. Relax your head and your neck. Take a few deep breaths. And keep breathing out all your negative energies.

Disconnect from Negativities...
Now say in your mind, *"Disconnect from people (you may say the names of specific people if there are any), from negative entities, events and situations".*

Then say, *"Disconnect at all three levels of physical, mental, and emotional."*

Take deep breaths and feel light as the negative connections disconnect from you.

Align with the planet...
You may bring your hands together in front of your chest like a Namaskar salutation and bow your head gently.

Say in your mind, *"I am grateful to our planet for giving me everything I need. I salute our planet and align with its energy."*

You may continue to keep your hands in the Namaskar salutation or place them on your knees with your palms facing upward.

Now feel the Earth's energy enter through your feet and rise to your legs and the rest of your body. If you feel a tingling sensation, allow the sensation to continue. If you are a visual person, visualize this energy entering through your feet and spreading inside every part of your body. Breathe deeply. Allow this energy to open your chakras.

Remain in this position until the Earth's energy has filled your body and energized your chakras.

Align with your purpose...
You may bring your hands together like a Namaskar salutation again and bow your head gently or say in your mind, *"I am grateful to the Universe for guiding me and for helping me through life. I salute my soul and align with its energy. Show me my true purpose, take me through my purpose. I am aligned with my soul. I have no fear or doubts and allow my soul to take me through my journey."*

Feel your soul's energy enter from the top of your head (your crown chakra). You may feel a tingling sensation on your head. Allow it. Allow your soul's energy to fill every part of your body.

If you are a visual person, you can see your soul's energy mix with the Earth's energy inside you.

Remain in this position for as long as you like. Feel the peace and calm within you.

Shield yourself...
Take a few deep breaths and visualize a protective transparent shield around you, at all three levels: physical, mental, and emotional.

Say in your mind, *"I command my shield to protect me from any negative energies, entities, negative people, situations, events. I command my shield to only allow positive energy to enter. I command it to remain for a week. I and I alone can take it down."*

Now take a deep breath and visualize your protective shield around you.

Slowly open your eyes and feel aligned with your soul. Smile!

Step 2: Do the value mapping exercise to understand your top 10 values. While they may not all connect with your true purpose, they will help you understand your priorities and your key drivers. This is important to understand prior to determining your true purpose.

Step 3: Ask yourself the following questions to better understand what you are passionate about. Our true purpose can be closely associated with our passion:

What would you do if you had only one more year to live and didn't care how much money you made? What work would you do?

What would you do if you had no concern about money? If you had an abundance of it from other sources?

What would you do to make money if you could pick your own job?

What would you want to be or do if you didn't care about what others thought of you (including your parents and friends)?

What would you do for work if you didn't have any responsibilities, such as family or debt?

What are you really good at? What comes to you naturally? Is there a skill or a type of work that is exciting, motivating, and something you truly enjoy or love doing?

Now, based on your answers above, what are your two picks? Do not think about whether you have the skills or the right network or the experience.
   1.

   2.

The above exercise is meant to give you a view of your passion and potentially help with determining one element of your true purpose.
   True purpose is comprised of two key elements:
   - Your strategic action
   - Your impact on the environment or beings of the

planet

Building a top firm is a goal but not true purpose. Creating the top grossing film is a goal but not true purpose. Traveling the world is a desire and goal but not true purpose. Purpose involves an additional element of impact of your actions on this world, its environment and beings.

You might ask what's in it for me? If you find your true purpose and align with it, you will find:

- The joy and peace you have been looking for
- An end to restlessness from not aligning with your purpose
- A true sense of appreciation and value, not just from yourself but also from others.

Step 4: Identify your impact statement
Answer the following questions:

Is there a cause (human, animal, plants, environmental) that you feel most connected to?

Are there any groups of people or organizations you feel most connected to?

If you were able to donate money, who would you donate to? Any specific causes?

What is the one challenge in this world or challenges in this world that you feel strongly about eliminating?

If you had time to volunteer what type of work would you volunteer for?

Where do you think you can make the biggest impact in society or for the environment?

If doing something for someone or a group of people would make you happy, what would it be?

If you struggle with identifying causes that you connect with, here is what you can do. Pick three non-profit organizations dealing with three different causes. If you have a favorite animal or feel strongly about a social cause, pick an organization that aligns with it. Let's say I love cats, one of my picks may be an organization that shelters abused cats. Another may be dealing with homeless people and a third may be dealing with youth programs. Pick three whose cause you most connect with.

Visit each of them on three different weekends. Spend half a day or a few hours, depending on your schedule. I can guarantee you a feeling of joy for the entire duration of your volunteering activity. Some may even feel emotional. If you feel joy while you are at work, then it is a sign that you connect with the cause. This does not mean you have to quit your job and join the non-profit organization, unless that is what you truly wish to do.

Based on what you have filled in the blanks above, what are your two picks?
1.

2.

For instance, some of you may be passionate about airplanes, trains, bridges, or physical structures. You may be an engineer or designer or an architect and come up with ideas that reduce materials or carbon footprints, thereby helping the environment. That can become your true purpose.

Some of us are lucky to find our passions at an early age and if you are one of them, you must seek out your true purpose. Ask yourself how you can use your passion to give back to the five kingdoms on the planet. Most importantly, you must pursue your passion. Every truly successful person does.

Step 5: Aligning strategic action with impact
From Steps 2 and 3 above, fill in the blanks

Your strategic action statements:
1.

2.

Your impact statements:
1.

2.

Can you connect any of your strategic action statements with your impact statements? Can your strategic actions lead to any of your impact statements?
Example: Strategic action statement: *Provide tools and*

techniques to develop life and leadership skills
Impact statement: *Empower children and youth.*

True Purpose: *To empower children and youth with leadership and life skills by providing tools and techniques that help them achieve a fulfilled life.*

Example: Strategic action statement: *Build and run a technology company*

Impact statement: *Empower children in need of education in third world countries.*

True Purpose: *To build a technology company that is focused on creating platforms to bring affordable and free education to children in third world countries.*

Your Strategic action statement:

Your Impact statement:

Your True Purpose:

Step 6. Action planning and next steps
The final step is the action plan. If my purpose is to eradicate cruelty to cats, how do I go about it? I could volunteer at the cat shelter, I could help create marketing programs. I'm a management consultant, so I could offer to help make their organization more robust or efficient. I could offer to consult for free in areas where they are challenged. If I were a musician, I might even write a song about cats or sing to them or play music to them. Some might laugh but if you are a musician and a cat lover, I think you know what I mean. If you are a photographer, you could offer to take pictures of cats that

can be put up on the website to attract people who might want to adopt them. Provide your services in whichever way you can. Be creative. It is not always about donating money but if that is what you wish to do, so be it.

Action 1:

Action 2:

Action 3:

As you go through this step, refer back to your top 10 values. Evaluate whether your true purpose aligns with your value map. Not all values will be impacted by the true purpose, but this is an important check-point to determine the actions you will take. If the actions do not align with any of your values, then there is a need to revisit your value exercise. It is rare that one's true purpose is not aligned with one's value map.

#	Values (from your value map)	Impact of above actions (+/-)
1		
2		
3		
4		
5		
6		
7		
8		
9		

10	

Some of my clients come to me with questions about their careers and jobs. They don't want to find their true purpose, even though I recommend it. For those who're looking for a way to determine their next step or next job, here is a simple exercise for you.

Tool #10: Determine your next job
This is similar to the value exercise we did in the previous chapter. Some may be able to use their top five values and skip steps one and two below. However, I recommend you do steps one and two because I've come across individuals whose aspirations end up being different from their top five values. The aspirations are also at a slightly different level to values:

Step 1: Make a list of your aspirations for your professional work. For example, they may be:
- Enough time to go on vacations
- Enough money to stabilize my finances
- Opportunities to grow and learn
- Work from home
- Work in consulting

1.	
2.	
3.	
4.	
5.	
6.	
7.	

8.	
9.	
10.	

Read them and update them as needed.

Step 2: Your aspirations may align with your top ten values. Cut down your list above to your top five using the technique we had used to prioritize your top ten values.

For example, using the example in step one, would ask the question, do I want to have enough money to stabilize my finances or do I want to have enough time to go on vacations?

Do I want to have enough money to stabilize my finances or do I want to work from home when I want to?

Do I want to have enough money to stabilize my finances or do I want to change careers to consulting?

Do I want to have enough time to go on vacations or do I want to work from home when I want to?

Do I want to work from home when I want to or do I want to work in consulting?

A1.
A2.
A3.
A4.
A5.

As an example, let's assume, you picked:
A1) Finances

A2) Opportunity to learn
A3) Location ~ US/NZ,
A4) Proximity to family (New Jersey, Texas)
A5) Career growth in international markets

Step 3: Now, make a list of all aspirational roles you would like to adopt. Include at least three options based on your current skill set and three that go beyond your skills. Try to be as specific as possible.
Examples:
R1: I want to be an editor in a US publishing firm
R2: I want to be a senior manager in consulting for the media industry in New Zealand

R1.
R2.
R3.
R4.
R5.
R6.

Step 4: Next, pick your top three from the list above. If you have two or three in your list, that is fine too. If you have one, then you've already figured it out. Map them to your top five aspirations or values (whichever you have picked to do this exercise).

Example:

Roles	A1	A2	A3	A4	A5
R1. I want to work as an editor with a US publisher	5	7	10	10	3
R2. Sr. Manager in consulting for media in NZ	8	8	8	0	5

Totals: R1-35 and R2-29.

These examples were fairly extreme but can give you a sense of how to score your options. If you have created your value map, use it to weigh your options.

Roles	A1	A2	A3	A4	A5
R1.					
R2.					
R3.					

Totals: R1- _____ R2- _____ R3- _____

Focus on your top two, network with the people in those industries and apply for jobs.

This brings us to the end of five key pillars of becoming your own Superhero. We began this journey with understanding how wishes work and why the need to align with one's true purpose. Then we delved into emotions and patterns, and used tools to deal with them. Tools to deal with fears, tools to let go and rely on the Universe, find joy in the path and not be attached to outcomes, become resilient. The next couple of chapters helped us understand who we truly are and our true values. These values, in conjunction with our true purpose, sets our success metrics.

The following final four chapters introduce concepts and theories based on my understanding and research from various Eastern and Western sources. While some of the theories may be fairly esoteric in nature, I want to share them with you. I believe there is much to be discovered in this space, and as we enhance our group consciousness, we will begin to unravel many of the Universe' secrets and fascinating truths. These theories are for those who question and are curious about what might be. For those who are open to energy sciences and esoteric possibilities.

11 THEORY: COMPLEX WEB

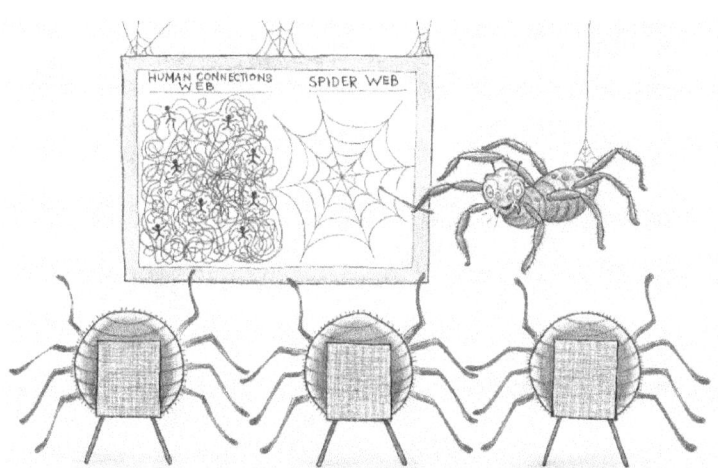

Remember, this is the web that will bring you flies...
the human one will only bring you stress...

Jolly Wally Marriage Blues
After forty years of marriage, an old Jolly Wally shaved his head and left home to see a monk.

"My wife has made my life hell for the past forty years. I can't take it anymore. I have come to you to become a monk. Please make me your disciple."

"What have you done to your wife to deserve such behavior?" said the monk calmly.

"I must have tortured her in a past life. She has tortured me for the past forty years."

The monk nodded.

"You were a snake in a past life and your wife was a sparrow. She laid eggs every season and you would crawl up the tree and eat them. For many seasons, this continued. As a snake it is not your fault – you eat bird eggs. But after years of not being able to have any children, the sparrow died in sorrow."

The Jolly Wally looked puzzled. "I wasn't serious when I said I may have tortured her in a past life."

"I wasn't being serious when I said you were a snake. But every time you do get annoyed, think of the poor sparrow and forgive her. You could be the sparrow next birth."

The old Jolly Wally laughed and returned home to make peace with his wife.

***

Theory of Karma
Let's say you can learn the lessons you need to reach your goals or related to your karma through specific types of events and situations. There may be other people in this world who can also use those same events and situations to learn their own lessons, which may or may not be different from yours. The situation or event is the same, but the lessons may vary. Then the Universe will bring you together with those other people so you can both learn and grow.

Assume that I have a lesson of acceptance to learn in matters of self-love. My friend Angela has a lesson of forgiveness to learn in matters of love. Angela and I get together and start seeing each other but it doesn't work out. In the process, I learn to accept myself for who I am, and Angela learns to forgive me for breaking up with her. Both of us needed the same situation and while we both felt sadness and anger, our core lessons were different. This is an example of a simpler version of how the Universe connects people.

Throw in a slight complication. Assuming that there is a person in the set of other people mentioned above, who has a past life connection with me. This person is not Angela. In that case, I will meet this other person first and neutralize my karma with the person. When it is done, we part ways, I get my lesson of acceptance and self-love.

However, if I haven't fully learned my lesson to reach my goal of being in a long-term relationship, the Universe may then bring me together with Angela, if she too hasn't learned her lesson of forgiveness.

If I did learn to love myself unconditionally while I was with the other person, then I may remain with the other person and not meet Angela at all. Or even if I meet her, we may just be friends and never date.

I set my goal of being in a long-term relationship. The ability to assess and realize the lessons is mine. The ability to learn the lesson is also mine. The connecting with people and situations rests with the Universe, enabling me to learn my lessons. Do you see how this theory of karmic connections works?

Theory of Homophily

There is another theory about why we meet certain people in our lives. Numerous experiments have been conducted on this topic. Without getting into the details of the social experiments, the gist is that we connect with people who are like us, share similar taste in music, have similar ethical values, religious values, etc. Have you noticed how we befriend people of similar spiritual inclinations and similar mental wavelengths? Some call it wavelength, others call it energy. Like attracts like.

It is possible to also combine the two theories mentioned above. Where the Universe considers three key elements when connecting people: 1) past life karma, 2) similar interest groups, 3) similar events/situations needed to learn lessons. So, if Angela shares some past life karma with me and we share similar interests in spirituality and values, and we need to go through the same event or situation to learn our lessons, then she will be the first person I meet. There can of course be many Angelas for me in this world and vice-versa. Complex connections and web indeed.

It is interesting to note that many of the lessons we need to learn will be similar to those of our parents. This is because we may have many traits in common. We may be stubborn and need to learn to accept. We may be impatient and need to learn to be patient. I have certainly seen many common lessons between me and my brother, and my parents.

Irrespective of the theory on how the Universe brings us together with other people, it is important that we appreciate and acknowledge those who have helped us in our lives. Many times, we bump into random people who end up helping us with no motive for gain. Take a moment to thank them in your thoughts. Use the gratefulness practices and meditations. And welcome more positivity to yourself.

12 THEORY: PARTNER IN CRIME OR PARTNERS IN CRIME

When Wishes Come True

A Jolly Wally woman and her Jolly Wally husband were married for a few years when she started to notice his constant bickering and complaining. At first, she tried to tell him to look at the positive side of things but there was always something wrong and she eventually gave up.

"Wish someone would cook tasty meals for us," said the husband, after dinner one night.

Our Jolly Wally woman bit her tongue and reminded herself not to argue. She had cooked dinner that night.

"Wish someone would give me a massage. I'm so tired," complained the man, one evening when he returned from work.

"Do you want me to rub your shoulders?" said the woman.

The man shook his head.

"I think I need a professional massage," he said.

The wife shrugged and left the room.

"Wish someone would drive me to work today. I don't feel like driving," complained the man.

One evening, the Jolly Wally man returned home from work, to find three young and ruggedly handsome Jolly Wallys.

"Who are you... where is my wife?" he said with a puzzled look in his eyes.

"You know I agree with you," said his wife from behind the men.

"Perhaps it is true that one person cannot be everything. And I thought about all the problems you've been having. I reminded myself that I must be a good companion and wife and think about your needs so here are the three men."

She introduced them as their cook, masseur, and chauffeur. The husband looked shocked.

"But we don't have that kind of money to pay for such luxuries," he whispered to his wife.

The woman laughed.

"You don't have to worry about that. They are for free. They are my lovers."

"What?"

"One of them has the most amazing body... so beautiful and chiseled... Sigh! He's also a great cook. The other one is so charming and is constantly complimenting me. He will be our masseur and he is

professional — just like you like it. The third one... well, he is just a sweet one and will drive you on days you don't feel like driving yourself."

The husband stared at his wife in disbelief.

"But I'm only trying to be helpful, darling. Hopefully, they will meet your needs and wishes too," she said with a smirk.

***

Theory of Constraint

Each one of us sets out on a journey based upon our aspirations and goals, intertwined with our karmic lessons. The journey is full of situations and events that allow us to learn and grow. Some of us have lessons that are so diverse and complex that one partner may not be able to fulfill this need. In this case, you may meet several lovers who can help you through your journey by creating events and situations that help you grow. Your lessons may be in the matters of trust, respect, and love, key ingredients of a relationship. There may also be other lessons related to self-esteem, confidence, stress management, anger management, and so on, that you need to learn to enhance your professional life. It is possible that one lover is unable to provide you with all the lessons you need to achieve your objectives. While you could learn these lessons through friends or family, your love relationships may be the fastest way for you to learn. This is where you ask yourself whether you must be angry with the person/s who broke your heart or instead forgive and thank them for helping you grow.

While I was in the Himalayas, watching the sunset one evening, I felt a sudden cool breeze as it settled over my face and I found myself taking a deep breath of relief. My mind wandered to thank the Universe for allowing me this wonderful trip to the Himalayas. And then it wandered to my last relationship. I realized that I would have never had the chance to make this trip or to grow mentally and emotionally like I did unless we had broken up. At that instance I realized that I was not angry at my ex-partner but was grateful for helping me grow.

Theory of Patterns
Another explanation for dating different people but not finding 'The One' can be a pattern, especially if the emotional experience you face in each relationship is similar. Then you must find out what you need to learn from this pattern. What habits, thoughts, or behaviors you need to change? Have the courage to unlearn your habits and allow yourself to change. This will help you break the pattern faster--unless you are happy to wait till the pattern runs its course and leaves you exhausted. I have already explained why we go through patterns. Use the technique in the chapter, 'Don't patent your patterns', to break patterns related to your love relationships.

Theory of Karma
A third explanation for not finding a partner is that you may have negative karma with many people in the area of love and affection (current life, or as per Eastern beliefs, past lives). And you may need to go through experiences of heartbreak with multiple people to neutralize this negative karma. When you do, you will be ready for a relationship and you'll find a partner – if you want one.

Have you wondered how it would be if you went back to one of your past romantic relationships? I am not talking about your first childhood love or your high school flame but someone you have dated as an adult. We tend to crave the positive emotions of love we felt in past relationships. But most times, it is the emotion and not the person we crave. Our minds have a hard time de-personifying emotion. It is okay to miss the emotion but be careful about missing the person who may have been wrong for you—you may have had all the right reasons to break away.

Many judge people who have not been in steady relationships or have gone from one partner to another and comment on how it is their fault that they cannot keep a relationship, how they're too picky or too flirty. What they fail to recognize is that such people probably want to be in a relationship but struggle with them. Many of these people recognize that their challenges lie within themselves but are unable to rectify them. They would appreciate if you put aside your judgments and comments and instead showed some compassion. It is the same with those who have addictions. It is true that those who are addicted are unable to break away from them and perhaps they do bad things to keep up their addictions. Be thankful to the Universe that you do not have addictions and show compassion towards those who are struggling. They are trying to their best of abilities. Remember, some of it is also caused by karmic associations in this lifetime and those from past lives. Even if you don't believe in past life karma, just train yourself to be more tolerant of those who are not as lucky as you and have compassion for their journeys.

A Superhero recognizes that we are all connected to one energy ecosystem and having compassion towards others also means showing compassion to yourself. It is the same as love.

13 THEORY: KNOCK! KNOCK!

Who's there?
Family!
That's impossible!
Why?
Mine never knocks!
That's my family… and there are three reasons I was born into it.

Reason 1. I have strong past life connections with my parents, my brother, and my extended family.

I underwent a session of past life regression to better understand my karmic connections with my family. The regression therapy helped me understand why I have certain fears. It was intense and I'm aware that not everyone is open to the concept of past lives or regression therapy, but it certainly helped me understand why I have a certain type of relationship with specific people in this lifetime.

Reason 2. By being born into my family, I have acquired their energetic (and genetic) dispositions, am influenced by my surroundings, have formed a personality that has allowed me to create situations, and put myself into situations so I can learn my life lessons to attain my true purpose and/or neutralize any negative karmas. We covered this topic in the chapter, 'Karma is… what?'. In short, I believe my family has provided me with the perfect setting for me to grow. I am happy with my life and where I am, so why look back into the past and regret what we cannot change? As long as we have learned from our challenges and our mistakes. Why go back and blame our parents?

I have compassion for those who have had difficult childhoods and have had abusive parents. I have seen how it impacts the lives of children and continues into their later years. If you are one of them, I hope you give yourself credit for how far you've come. I hope the tools and techniques in this book have helped you gain closure and move on from past traumas and emotions. I hope they have empowered you to move forward.

Many of us have been brought up in homes that are troubled and many decided to leave and find their own way through life. Many returned to rebuild their relationships with their parents while others stayed away. No matter where you stand in the spectrum, follow your intuition and do what brings you peace. If that means you need to get away and gain your strength before you can return and deal with past situations, so be it. Or if that means you can better assist your parents by being away from them and not getting entangled into their daily challenges, so be it. There is no right or wrong, only what feels right for you. However, always remember that there is no running away from a lesson you need to learn. If you think you can run away from your family to escape a lesson, you are mistaken.

Let's say you needed to learn to stand up for yourself and your father's anger issues have pushed you to do so. However, his anger issues have also caused you difficulties and you decide to get away from him. This will allow you temporary relief, but you will still need to learn to stand up for yourself. The lesson will come to you from other sources, like work colleagues or your boss, maybe a love relationship or close friends. It may not be the exact situation you faced at home with your father, but it will drive similar emotions. The pattern will continue until you learn. It is up to you how and where you wish to learn the lesson.

For example, my ex-partner has some traits of my parents that I have struggled with but, fortunately for me, I recognized this, and I understood the lessons they were driving. The best approach for me then was to accept what the Universe has brought to me and allow it to guide me through my process of learning.

14 THEORY: THE JOURNEY

This chapter is fairly esoteric, especially to those who may have not experienced energy healings or concepts related to it. While this is a theory, I hope you will keep an open mind and enjoy the possibilities stated.

The Theory of Death
Two Jolly Wallys stood inside a tall lighthouse overlooking the ocean.
　First Wally: *What happens in the end?*
　Second Wally: *End? What end?*
　First: *After we die.*
　Second: *What happens?*
　First: *We die but...*
　(pause)
　Second: *But?*
　First: *What happens to us after that?*
　Second *(to himself)*: *There he goes again!*
　First: *Interesting question, isn't it?*
　Second *nods.*
　First: *I bet you want to know, don't you?*
　Second: *Only if you...*
　First: *...only if I can answer this question? But why do you want to know? How will you use this knowledge?*
　Second: *I don't...*
　First: *... know the answer. I know you don't and you want to.*
　Second: *No! I don't! Stop! trying to finish my sentences.*
　First *laughs.*
　Second: *Why're you laughing? I didn't even...*
　First: *...answer it? So why don't you try to answer for a change. You've been quizzing me all evening.*
　Second: *Are you out of your mind?*
　First: *I am the wise one I know. But if you don't try, how will you get to it? A wise man once said...*

　He could not finish his sentence. The second grabbed his legs and held him over the edge of the tower.

　"*Did he say... go find out for yourself what happens when we die?*" *said the second one.*

　"*Let go!*" *shouted the first one.* "*No! don't let go!*"
　Second *(grinning)*: "*Make up your mind.*"

***

That was not the end for the Jolly Wally but before you want to hang me by my legs, I'll answer the question. To do so, I need to introduce the concept that we are energy. A simple experiment of observing the composition of an atom shows infinitely small vortices of energy. These are quarks and photons that make up the structure of an atom. The atom is not physical structure but made from invisible energy and mostly physical space. So, if we are mostly energy and space then how do we perceive our bodies through our touch and eyes? This is because our atoms are vibrating at certain frequencies. Our eyes and other senses are tuned to visualize these frequencies. This frequency of vibration and the space between atoms dictates how we perceive an element as solid, liquid, or gas.

Nikola Tesla has said, *"The day science begins to study non-physical phenomena, it will make more progress in one decade than in all the previous centuries of its existence."*

So, if our bodies are energy, our brains are energy, our thoughts are energy, our spirits are energy, so is our consciousness. Then the Earth too is energy and we are all part of its energetic ecosystem. Dr. Lynne McTaggart's book The Field is an excellent read if you want to understand how leading scientists, physicists, and biologists have experimented and concluded that we are all inside, and part of an energy field. The five kingdoms on the planet, namely, human, animal (insects, birds, fish, animals), plants, micro-organisms and minerals too are part of this energy ecosystem.

So, what happens when we die?

The spirit -- our energy connection to the planetary ecosystem disconnects from the physical body (also energy). The body is proclaimed dead while the spirit energy remains connected to the planet's ecosystem. Eastern texts suggest reincarnation of the spirit or soul when it is ready to connect to another body of energy (physical body). The concept of readiness brings the notion of a holding state between reincarnations. A holding state could be a heaven or hell as we call them. In either holding state, the soul undergoes energizing and reenergizing so it can connect with a body. The purpose of reenergizing is that energy is expended when a spirit connects or disconnects with a physical body (also energy but different kind of energy compared to the spirit energy).

One of my teachers and I conducted a series of experiments to test the above theory. We used muscle testing, a technique by which we connect with an individual's subconscious mind with permission from their subconscious mind, and request permission to ask questions to it. Through muscle testing of our fingers, we receive responses from their subconscious to ours – since we are all connected energetically. This technique is used by many healers today and muscle testing experiments have showcased how our body reacts to positive and negative energies. Since we are all connected with the energy ecosystem of the planet, we do have access to each other's consciousness. The day we start believing in this connectivity, we shall have more compassion on our fellow beings and refrain from causing harm to others. When we cause harm to others we also cause harm to ourselves since we are all connected. This aligns with the concept of karma where good karma returns to us a help and good things while negative karma created comes back to bite us. Or the phrase, as you sow, so you reap.

As part of our experiment, we tested the consciousness levels of individuals living and dead, mostly people we knew from different parts of the world and different walks of life. Many of them were family members and friends. The sample size was about thirty, of which about ten were deceased. You might wonder how we conducted a test on those deceased. You can seek permission from the deceased by intention, because they may be deceased from the physical realm, but their energies are part of the energetic ecosystem even if this person may have been reincarnated on the Earth. And we are all connected to this ecosystem. This concept may be foreign to many who have not experienced energy healing, and I can understand their apprehension toward such experiments and connections. However, for those open to such concepts, the experiment showed that all individuals have a higher level of consciousness energy when they are born and then this energy falls by the age of one. We can ask the subconscious about its levels at various ages. The energy levels continue to drop until they stabilize by age 18 to 25. After this, the energy levels move up or down but most people show an upward movement in their 30's and 40's. This gradual rise continues until their death (for those who are deceased). What is fascinating is that their consciousness levels just before death were similar to that at birth. In rare cases, the consciousness levels were higher than that during birth. My maternal grandfather's is one of them.

Our theory is that energy is expended during connection and disconnection between spirits and physical bodies. So, the energy lost after connection (birth) by year 1, would need to be built up prior to disconnection (death). Similarly, after disconnections (death), the spirit energy drops the need to re-energize, if it must reconnect with another physical body (reincarnation). To re-energize, it must go to a holding state that we have named heaven or hell. How this energizing or re-energizing takes place is not something I have delved into, but like our human lives, there must be a process. Many people fear death because of the unknown -- of what will happen to their spirit. I can understand their zest for life but I fail to understand this fear of death.

You might then ask, "Why does the spirit need to reconnect with a physical body again? Or a more important question -- why are humans on this planet at all?"

These two questions are interconnected. The Earth is an energetic being like all other planets. According to esoteric scripts, a planet's goal is to attain higher levels of energy and consciousness. It does so through the transformation of energy. This transformation takes place through beings that inhabit it – including plants, animals, minerals, micro-organisms, and humans. The goal of humans then becomes transformation of energy, elevation of energy and group consciousness.

You might then ask, "Why the need for such complexity of creating human life, giving them challenges and conflicts? Why would the Earth not come up with a simpler mechanism for transforming and elevating its energy?"

The Earth's energy is complex just like its ecosystem, and so my belief is that transforming it would also be a complex process. Perhaps this transformation requires complex beings like us, humans. We have a level of understanding and creativity that is not available to other kingdoms (plants, animals, microorganisms and mineral). We can analyse, interpret, learn concepts and ecosystems, experiment on them, build machines and technology and so much more. Unlike beings of other kingdoms on the Earth, we can create corporations and institutions, influence and share information across social media and formulate rules of the games we play. We have the ability to create positive energy and to transform negative energy to positive. This energy is part of the wider energy ecosystem of the planet. So, in essence we can help the planet to cleanse and transform its energy. The day we stop doing so, the planet will likely get rid of us. When humans understand and accept that the planet and nature are the governing body, I hope we will stop elevating our status above it. Stop creating more negative energy and focus on positivity.

This has been an era of change and many of us have felt it. The last decade has seen several changes and conflicts, and there are more to come. They will keep happening until we elevate our group consciousness and transform the energy of the planet collectively.

So, if we're here to help the planet, what's in it for us?

The more you help the planet and Universe, the more the planet and Universe will help you. It is a win-win situation. Align with them, trust them, and let go. Let them take you through the journey you truly deserve and help you become the Superhero you truly are.

Do you want abundance as you go through this journey of transforming energies for the planet?

Do you want to have a joyful experience as you go through it?

The Universe has all of what you want and more available

to you. It is up to you to work towards aligning and gaining access to this abundance.

This does not mean you have no control over your life. You absolutely do. There are various paths to take in your journey and you can pick and choose the ones that work for you. However, make sure you align your path toward enhancing the planet's energy. This can only be done by helping the five kingdoms on the planet. This is where your life's true purpose comes in. As part of the alignment, one must also work on himself or herself and remove the blockages we create in ourselves, through our emotions, our habits, our negative patterns. Do you see how all of it fits into the picture?

I hope this book has allowed you to question some of your experiences and thoughts. Also, question some of the thoughts suggested in the book. With curiosity and questioning, comes the need for understanding. Be more mindful of your experiences and look within yourself, instead of blaming others for your challenges and conflicts. My goal was to expose you to various tools, techniques and theories but it is up to you to pick and choose your own path. I am hopeful that this book has also helped you find and align with your values and true purpose. This alignment will connect you with the energy of the planet, irrespective of the path you choose. You will be able to use the planetary energy more frequently and more effectively to gain the abundance you truly deserve; make the most of the abundance and joy available to all of us.

I wish you the very best in unleashing your inner Superhero!

ABOUT THE AUTHOR

Ani has worked across continents in the US, Asia, Europe and New Zealand, taking up various leadership roles in Corporate while pursuing his passion for writing, psychology, coaching, energy meditations, and healing modalities.

During a sabbatical of 9 months in the Himalayas, living in ashrams and monasteries in India, he experienced powerful energy meditations and healings that led to the foundations of this book.

For the next ten years, he explored several tools and techniques and combined them with his corporate experience to create a simple and effective framework, one that he has successfully used to coach his teams and clients.

Ani believes in self-empowerment - you pick and choose from the tools and techniques he has provided in this book, weave them into your own story, share them with others and enjoy this journey of exponential growth. Just like he has.

www.ingramcontent.com/pod-product-compliance
Lightning Source LLC
Chambersburg PA
CBHW061322040426
42444CB00011B/2737